THE CASE
OF A
MIDDLE
CLASS
CHRISTIAN

Other books
by Charles Merrill Smith

How to Talk to God When You Aren't Feeling Religious
How to Become a Bishop without Being Religious
When the Saints Go Marching Out
The Pearly Gates Syndicate

THE CASE OF A MIDDLE CLASS CHRISTIAN

by
Charles
Merrill
Smith

WORD BOOKS, Publisher
Waco, Texas

THE CASE OF A MIDDLE-CLASS CHRISTIAN

Copyright © 1973 by Charles Merrill Smith

Printed in the United States of America
Library of Congress catalog card number: 73–84579

THIS IS FOR ART AND JUDY

Friends as close as family
for more than thirty years

CONTENTS

WHAT KIND
OF
CHRISTIANS
ARE WE
ANYWAY?

THAT'S EASY. We are Middle-Class Christians, most of us. In the United States and Canada, Christianity is almost wholly a middle-class affair. There is an American upper class, and some of its members are Christians, but numerically the upper class is of negligible size. The lower classes (a hateful phrase) tend to find a spiritual home among the vast offerings of sects and fringe groups available in our society.

However, the strong backbone of organized Christianity (the standard-brand churches) is middle class—upper-, middle-, and lower-middle class. The large, familiar denominations such as Presbyterian (both U.S. and U.S.A.), Protestant Episcopal, United Methodist, several Lutheran bodies, Baptist (American and Southern), and United Church of Christ are typical of what I call standard-brand churches. There are studies (such as Vance Packard's) which locate with precision the various denominations on the class scale.

The middle class owns these denominations, these standard-brand churches. The kind of religion preached and practiced in them, not surprisingly, is a reflection of

The Case of a Middle-Class Christian

middle-class perspectives and values. Middle-Class Christians think of their Christianity as normative.

Personally, I find it distasteful to put a modifier in front of Christian because I know that a modification is a sign of adulteration. When someone says "I am a conservative Christian" or "I am a liberal Christian," I know that some diluting solution has been injected into the bloodstream of the faith. That is why it pains me to admit that I am a Middle-Class Christian. How much of my Middle-Class Christianity is Christianity and how much of it is just middle class? This question bothers me, and it will bother you if you think about it.

The Middle-Class Christian has taken a pasting from critics in recent years. He is spiritually superficial, they say, and confuses his own cultural values with the demands of the faith. Theologically and biblically he's only semiliterate, and he conceives his faith to be little more than a list of petty moralisms. He has no deep commitment and shies away from bold ventures of the soul.

Hardly anyone troubles to point out the good things about the American Middle-Class Christian, perhaps because it is more fun to criticize than to praise. But there are good things to point out. He is the guy who has kept organized Christianity going. He pays the church's bills. He does not dog the responsibility of serving on boards, committees, fund drives—performing time-consuming, often boring tasks essential to keeping an enterprise afloat. By no means least, he is the one who sits in the pews Sunday after Sunday.

Both the charges against the Middle-Class Christian and the compliments to him are, in the main, accurate.

What would happen if you seriously scrutinized your Middle-Class Christian faith? What would it do to your faith if you honestly asked yourself what you really believe about God and Jesus and Christian behavior and per-

10

sonal commitment? Where would you end up if you tried
to harmonize the teachings of your religion with your
experience in the world?

You might end up right where you are now.

You might discard your faith.

Or you might, for the first time, discover what it is like
to believe something because you have thought it through
for yourself instead of just accepting what someone else
told you to believe.

I am convinced that all Middle-Class Christians should
seriously scrutinize their personal faith. Therefore I submit my own history of trying to find out what I really
believed as a stimulus for you to do likewise. My record
isn't systematic, or scientific, or anything like that. It is
just the history of how one Middle-Class Christian kept
trying to square his faith with experience.

The existentialists say that no one can take your bath
for you, and they are right. But sometimes you get a better
bath if someone else scrubs your back.

This is to help you scrub your back.

Chapter One

YOU
HAVE TO
BEGIN
SOMEWHERE

I AM A MIDDLE-CLASS CHRISTIAN. Maybe I am *the* Middle-Class Christian, meaning that I am as typical of the species as anyone can be. Anyway, I am typical enough.

I inherited my faith. I was the recipient of a cargo of ideas, attitudes, postures, values, convictions, affections, hostilities, and conformities. This collection was passed down to me by prior generations of evangelical Protestants and homogenized into a life style which I was assured was definitive—the definitive Christian pattern.

It would have been the same had I been born into a middle-class Roman Catholic home. Some of the ideas, loyalties, and cultural habits would have been different, but not all that different.

It was a closed-end faith. By *closed-end* I mean that those who held it assumed it was up to carrying a man along the admittedly detoured, potholed, and sometimes washed-out roadbed of life. No more information or light would be coming in because no more was needed. Christian preaching and teaching were glosses on the truth that had been given.

It was a precise and easily grasped configuration, this

inherited faith of mine. You could think of it as a football game. In fact, the analogy of the Christian life to a game was popular with preachers when I first became aware that I was a Christian by inheritance, and it still is.

You got on the team when you became an identifiable Christian—by baptism, a conversion experience, joining the church—the methods varied.

The playing field was life. The opposing team was captained by the devil. The defensive line was made up of the seven deadly sins, or some equivalent, and it defended the end zone toward which you were pushing, which was heaven. The devil's team huffed and puffed to push you back over the other goal line into hell. God was the referee who called the penalties, applied the rules, and decided who won and who lost.

The metaphor was a little mixed up, of course, because football is a team game, and Christian performance is scored on an individual basis. We got the point, though. The Christian life was a rough proposition, with the Christian pitted against a wily opponent and in constant danger of being scragged by temptation, penalized for violations of the rules, thrown for a big loss by a hard-charging sin. Your best defense was prayer, reading the Bible, regular church attendance, and cold showers.

When you are a kid, brought up this way and with all these patterns reinforced by your cultural environment, you don't question the picture of life they present. You might pick at it around the edges as I did. You might even say that this idea or that item doesn't make sense as I did. But you just assume that because your elders and betters hold to it, then it is the straight goods. And this is how a Middle-Class Christian gets hammered into shape. This is how you get started on being a Christian. This is what I mean by inheriting your faith.

What I have described, of course, is an oversimplified

version of the faith held by most Middle-Class Christians today, but not much oversimplified.

The Middle-Class Christian today, in the main, owns a more sophisticated model of the faith. Chrome has been added. Some of the body metal has been resculptured, and there is a wider choice of colors and upholstery. The Middle-Class Christian has been to college. He can now talk about the problem of evil instead of the devil, although he likely still believes in a personal devil. He has a more sophisticated view of sin or sins. It is possible that he now recognizes that his faith has a dimension of social responsibility, that saving souls isn't enough, although he very probably considers saving souls as the main business of the church.

But it's the same old picture of how life is that he has in his head. An outline of the Middle-Class Christian's mental image of what the world is like and how he is supposed to go about living in it usually includes the following assumptions:

1. God will be good to you if you are good to God because God is a person who watches over you and to whom you are accountable.

2. The Christian life is prescribed in rules, and the best Christian is the one who best keeps the rules.

3. The aim of the Christian life is personal salvation, a goal usually equated with qualifying for heaven.

4. We have to live in the world and do business in it, but the world should be regarded as temporary, transient, and inimical to spiritual values.

5. We are creatures of flesh and spirit, but the spiritual side of our nature is superior because that's the side God is interested in. We have to be wary of the physical side because it is always intruding on and inhibiting the development of the spiritual side.

6. God likes hard-working, aggressive people and re-

wards them for these qualities. He doesn't care much for lazy people and finds especially distasteful people who rely on others for their support.

7. The Euro-American, or Western, way of life is history's best example of Christian civilization, and the American version is best of all.

8. Jesus Christ is somehow our savior although we aren't too sure exactly what it is he saves us from and exactly what it is he saves us to.

9. Jesus Christ is also our example, but whether we are to imitate just his spirit, or whether we are to imitate his life of poverty, radical commitment to the Kingdom, selfless service, and a cross is a troublesome question which it is best not to worry about too much.

10. The Bible, the typical Middle-Class Christian knows, is somehow his supreme authority in matters of faith and morals because it is God's Word. But he isn't certain why it is God's Word, and he isn't too well acquainted with what is in the Bible.

11. A Christian should belong to and actively support one of the mainline churches (Presbyterian, Methodist, Baptist, Lutheran, Roman Catholic, and so on) because only the Christian church keeps Christian faith and culture going.

This is, I think, a fair and accurate profile of the Middle-Class Christian perspective. It describes the faith I inherited, and I am a typical MCC (let's abbreviate Middle-Class Christian since we will be using it a lot and it is boring to write it out over and over).

My inherited faith worked for me for awhile. During adolescence and just after, it hobbled me enough to prevent any disastrous personal conduct. At least I didn't get any girls pregnant, and I didn't become a public drunk.

It gave me a bag of values—honesty, uprightness, decency, kindness—with which to structure my life. I didn't always live up to these values, of course, but their violation was accompanied by a sense of failure and a determination to try harder.

And my inherited faith lent a sense of overall meaning to life. It taught me that some kind of worthy service to others is the best kind of life investment.

So my inherited faith served me well—at first. It probably would be serving me well today had I remained in an uncomplicated rural environment and if the world hadn't changed abruptly. But I didn't, and the world did.

Because I found myself living in a more complex environment and because the world wouldn't hold still and behave itself, I found that my inherited faith simply wouldn't hold up under the altered circumstances, the new pressure. It wasn't strong enough; it wasn't good enough; it just wasn't adequate.

So what do you do with a faith that cracks, buckles, and tears under strain?

You can pretend that it is still O.K.

You can discard it.

You can patch it up.

Or you can reappraise it, try to see if maybe there is more to it than you thought, that maybe you hadn't got it quite right.

The last option was my choice. I had inherited enough Christian conviction to believe that my faith provided me with the right handle on life. But I was realist enough to admit that I hadn't gotten a good hold on that handle.

The reappraisal went on for years and is still going on. This has not always been a pleasant experience, for it doesn't always come out where I want it to come out.

For a long time I thought I was unique, that I was the only MCC trying to square his faith with the reality of his expanding experience, trying to stretch his faith to

17

cover the facts of his life. That, of course, was a conceit. Millions of American Middle-Class Christians are uninterested in asking any questions of their faith. There are other millions of MCCs, though, who are ready, willing, and anxious to haul out their questions and ask them.

Let's haul them out.

Chapter Two

YOU'VE GOT
TO BE
HONEST

A FEW YEARS AGO a nationally prominent preacher, delivering the Easter sunrise sermon at one of those spectacular services they stage in California, stated to the congregation assembled and to the presumed millions of sleepy Christians who had dutifully tuned in on the radio: "The resurrection of Jesus Christ is the best-attested fact in human history."

That's dishonest.

It is dishonest because it simply isn't true. We have only four accounts of the resurrection, those found in the Gospels, and they are not in agreement. And anyway, the Gospels were not written as objective history. Their purpose was to preach a message. They do not furnish us with hard historical evidence.

You may by now be hurling epithets at me—heretic, Bible disbeliever, corrupter of the faith, and such (which I deny)—but that has nothing whatever to do with my assertion that the sunrise preacher was dishonest. It may well be that the resurrection happened pretty much like the Gospels say it did. Something happened to rejuvenate the disheartened and dispersed disciples of Jesus. Their

19

The Case of a Middle-Class Christian

Lord being raised from the dead would surely have accomplished their rejuvenation. But this is not historical evidence. It is an informed surmise.

You may say, "Well, the Bible attests to the resurrection, and I believe the Bible." Fine. Many excellent Christian people share your confidence in the Bible's literal accuracy. But that is a belief, not evidence. You have to learn to call things by their right names. We should respect any man's sincerely held belief, but neither he nor we should pretend that his belief is the same thing as evidence.

The sunrise preacher said that the resurrection of Jesus Christ was buttressed by hard historical evidence. That is a statement capable of being either true or false, and it is demonstrably false. Had he said, "Today, we witness to our faith that on the third day Christ rose from the dead, as we are assured by the Gospels," then no one could have quarreled with him. Belief in the resurrection is a part of the Christian faith. On Easter Sunday Christians gather to celebrate and witness to their faith. And the Gospels tell us quite clearly that this is what happened.

So the sunrise preacher either lied, and knew he was lying, or he didn't understand the difference between belief and evidence—probably the latter. So I can't really blame him too much. It was a long time before I had a glimmer that there is a difference between belief and evidence. And I was longer yet learning that when it comes to considering the questions and problems arising from your religious faith you have to be honest in the way you handle them—absolutely honest.

My problem was that I had an emotional bias in favor of the Christian faith. Still have, for that matter.

And so do you.

If you are a hard-line evangelical or Roman Christian (a pejorative term, maybe, but descriptive of a large block of MCCs), then you defend fiercely against any intimation that a single thread in the fabric of your faith won't quite pass an objective inspection. For you, to pull out one thread is to tear it.

The vaster number of us MCCs, though, sit a bit looser in the saddle. For whatever reason, we accept the inspection of ideas. We are open, some of us more and some of us less, to the possibility of new insights. Most of us are even willing to shift from previously held positions of faith should new light shine the way. But all of us are somewhat defensive about any kind of attack on our faith. Even that species which is the object of homiletical diatribes and missionary cajolery, the nominal Christian, is not indifferent to attacks on Christendom. He doesn't understand much about Christianity maybe, and he isn't going into the trenches to defend it. But his culture, moral pretensions, and political philosophy are all tied up with Christianity, and any threat to it is a threat to him—or at least he thinks it is.

All of us Middle-Class Christians, then—from the fundamentalist, through the mildly affiliated, to the liberal humanist—have some emotional investment in the faith. To some degree, admittedly more intense for some than for others, we want it to be true.

For me the problem was further complicated by my choice of the Christian ministry as a vocation. Have you ever pondered how unpleasant is the position of the preacher who attempts to handle honestly the questions arising from the faith he is paid to extol? His job analysis says he is there to promote the faith, not examine it. Oh, he may pretend to examine it. He may announce a sermon subject such as "Are the Ten Commandments Out of Date?" But he knows, and so does the congregation, that his answer had better be "No, they are not out of date," or there will be a hastily called meeting of the pulpit committee to consider the termination of his contract.

A reasonable case can be made that this is how it ought to be. If the professional parish clergyman doesn't embrace an acceptable version of the faith (acceptable to his congregation and to his ecclesiastical superiors), then he ought to teach school or sell insurance, or—if he must preach—hire a hall out of his own pocket. Nobody compels him to be a preacher. If he thinks the acceptable version of the faith won't balance under careful audit, he ought to split. Incidentally, this is happening. The rather spectacular numbers of parish clergymen, especially Roman Catholics, now heading for the exits includes not a few who can't buy acceptable versions of the faith any longer and are doing the honorable thing.

If he doesn't chuck it, though, the parish clergyman has to be careful about being honest with questions related to the faith. He'd better believe it is true, or he'll get ulcers trying to convince people it is true. He'd better see that his congregation believes it is true, or he's out of business.

What I'm trying to say to Middle-Class Christians is that the obstacles to an honest evaluation of our inherited faith are formidable for all of us. Start on that assumption, or you won't get in field-goal range of honesty. I put in the bit about preachers to show you I had a double burden on honesty because I had a vocational stake in institutionalized faith. It also reveals my continuing bias. I want to be honest, and honesty compels me to admit that I want it to turn out that the Bible is sufficient for faith and life, that the church—in the face of much evidence to the contrary—is still relevant and worthwhile, and that the Christian way, properly understood, is the best way. You should read me with the knowledge that I won't be able to separate myself from my personal history, and sometimes that history will be an impediment to objectivity.

So how do you go about being honest with your faith questions?

Well, I can only tell you how I began. At a point now lost in some valley or forest of my memory I became aware that many of the faith questions being posed for me were masking the real questions. Let me give you an example.

I recall that at a Christian youth conference I attended there was a hot discussion group on the topic of what games Christians could play with a good conscience. The group leader, a pudgy middle-aged clergyman, pronounced the following answers as if they were writ on stone somewhere:

Is it permissible for a Christian to play bridge?
No.
Is it permissible for a Christian to play Old Maid?
Yes, but never on Sunday.

This all seems quaint and ridiculous at this late date and seemed so to me at the time. It was years before I realized that these silly questions with their trivial answers masked a serious and important question: Is there a distinctive Christian life style?

Take another example. One faith question which was always being asked, preached over, bruited about, and used as the test of authentic faith when I was a young man (and still is in many Christian quarters) was this: Was Jesus born of a virgin?

Although as an adolescent anything having to do with sex was interesting to me, I thought this was a pretty dumb question. And it is a pretty dumb question. So two of the four Gospels say that Jesus was born of a virgin. So what? The other two don't mention it. What do I care about the mechanics of Jesus' birth? What does that have to do with the real Jesus?

The Case of a Middle-Class Christian

But all the foofaraw about the virgin birth masks the real question: Was Jesus essentially different in some way from all other men, and if so, how? Ironically, as I discovered a good many years later, while today we use the virgin birth tradition to prove that Jesus was different, that he was divine, the early church used it to prove that Jesus was the same as other men, that he was human. Nobody in those days argued about his divinity. They all assumed it. But there were Christians who insisted that Jesus was in no sense human, and the church said, "That just ain't so, and we can prove by the Gospels that though his conception was divine his birth was natural and normal in every way. So he was truly human as well as truly divine."

So, for me, the first step in handling faith questions honestly was learning to peel back the questions posed and find the real question underneath.

You still hear, in Christian circles, much commotion over the question, Is the Bible to be accepted as the literally accurate Word of God? I have heard it argued, one way and another, all my life and still am hearing it. As this is written, one of the large, established, and quite respectable denominations is tearing itself apart over just this issue.

Now it strikes me, and probably you, that this question is hardly worthy of so much attention—a conviction supported by the silly statements always generated in the heat of the battle over it. And indeed it isn't worthy of all that intellectual sweat.

But the verbal accuracy of the Bible isn't the real question. The real question being asked is, What is the ultimate authority for the Christian, and if it is the Bible, how dependable an authority is it? That's a question to which the literal accuracy of the Bible is only a minor footnote. That's a question well worth some pondering.

24

Should the Presbyterian church have contributed, as it did, a substantial sum of money to the defense fund for Angela Davis, an avowed Communist? Maybe it should have, or maybe it shouldn't have. It is futile, however, to ask that question. The question is, Should the church help people in trouble, and if so, how does it choose the recipients of its benefactions?

For me, learning to unmask the real questions was the first giant step toward an honest evaluation of my inherited faith, and I believe it is where you ought to begin. It will save you from fooling around on the sidelines when the action is out on the field.

Then, I had to learn to respect facts.

Sure, you say, that's important. Everyone should respect facts. It's smart to be smart.

I know you respect facts. You respect facts when you buy a car or build a house or accept a job. You think you respect facts in handling faith questions too, but you don't.

Did you ever reflect on how we Middle-Class Christians hedge against facts when they concern our faith? We try to keep the adherents of our particular brand of Christianity from exposure to facts that would contravene and undermine our cherished doctrines. This is one reason that denominations have their own colleges. One of the ideas behind the Christian college (and one that elicits financial support from the faithful) is that it will shepherd the Christian students committed to its care through the maze of facts so that they will come out—so far as their faith is concerned—just where they went in.

A part of this business of handling faith questions honestly is admitting that we are wary of facts which threaten some strongly held item in our list of beliefs.

Take an example. A friend of mine preached a Christmas sermon in which he said, among other things, that

25

the angels and shepherds and manger and strange star composed a lovely poetic statement of the early church's faith. Only the language of poetry, he said, is capable of conveying this kind of truth, this kind of meaning. So, he said, we should treat the nativity stories not as history but as poetry.

Well, you would have thought he had attacked motherhood or the oil depletion allowance. The congregation, substantial parts of it anyway, wanted to run him out of the ministry. The preacher himself was shocked at the violent reaction (he was young and naïve) because he thought he was saying something good and supportive of the Christian faith, but his congregation thought he was saying something bad and destructive.

So the people challenged him: Are you denying the truth of the nativity stories?

Not at all, he replied. He wasn't denying anything. He was only saying that these stories should be read as poetry, as a reverent statement of faith, rather than as history.

But the stories were in the Gospels and that made them history, they said.

No, he said, the Gospels weren't objective history. They were written as Gospels, which is to say they were written to proclaim a message. This was easy to demonstrate, and, so far as he knew, no one, not even the most conservative Christian scholar, disputed that in the Gospels the message, not the history, was primary. Therefore, the Gospel writers often used nonhistorical material—oral tradition, poetic imagery, and so on—to proclaim their message. This was also easy to demonstrate.

But why, they asked him, did he say the nativity stories were not history? Why couldn't they be history as well as poetry?

Well, he replied, it is unlikely that they could have been

history because we know for a fact (easily verifiable) that the early church had no interest whatever in Jesus' birth until long after his death, when the facts of his birth were not recoverable. After all, Mark, the writer of the original Gospel, thought the manner of Jesus' birth of so little consequence that he did not include an account of it.

But isn't it a fact, they asked, that God inspired Matthew and Luke to write the nativity stories exactly like it happened?

That is not a fact, he said, that is a belief.

The people weren't satisfied. They could not refute the pastor's position, but they felt threatened by it. They didn't defrock him, of course, but he soon moved on to other fields of service, as the euphemism goes. The Christian people of this particular congregation may have been pious, full of good works, and exemplars of Christian behavior. But they did not respect facts.

Or maybe their trouble was that they had never learned to distinguish facts from beliefs. Most of us MCCs mix up facts and beliefs until the two are inseparable in our minds.

What's the difference between a fact and a belief? Facts are data, or occurrences, or history that are supported by evidence which is strong enough to eradicate any reasonable doubt as to their authenticity.

Beliefs are history, a point of view, a conviction, a theory, an explanation, or a philosophy which may or may not be supported by evidence, but which cannot be verified as accurate beyond a reasonable doubt.

For example: It is a fact that President Abraham Lincoln was murdered in a box at Ford's Theater in Washington, D.C., by a pistol shot. Since no one is now alive who witnessed the event, how can we say this is a fact?

Because we have voluminous records of the event—newspaper stories, eyewitness accounts, medical testimony

—which are in substantial agreement as to what happened. No reasonable man doubts this.

It is a belief that President Abraham Lincoln was assassinated by an actor named John Wilkes Booth. This belief is supported by some evidence. One can make out a strong case that the belief is accurate. But there is not enough evidence to say that Booth, beyond any reasonable doubt, was the guilty man. It is still an hypothesis, a belief.

There is no reasonable alternative to the statement, "President Abraham Lincoln was murdered in a box at Ford's Theater in Washington, D.C." There are reasonable alternatives to the statement, "President Lincoln was assassinated by an actor named John Wilkes Booth."

And that's the difference between a fact and a belief.

So if you want to be honest in handling questions of faith, you have to learn to call things by their right names. Or to put it another way, don't do what most MCCs do, which is to call a belief a fact.

Christian doctrines, for example, shouldn't be called facts. Christian doctrines are formulations of what Christians (or those Christians who formulated the doctrines) believe. None of them are supported by enough evidence to remove every reasonable alternative. Perhaps we should say none of them with the exception of the doctrine of original sin. As the late G. K. Chesterton pointed out, the doctrine of original sin, properly stated and properly understood, is the one Christian doctrine which can be demonstrated as accurate beyond any reasonable doubt.

The doctrine of the Holy Trinity may well be accurate, but there is no conceivable way of demonstrating its accuracy this side of Judgment Day.

The Christian doctrine of the atonement (or one of them—there are several, and the church never did settle on one as official) may reflect reality, but there is no conclusive evidence that this is the case.

I, personally, am convinced that the doctrine of salvation by grace through faith is true. But that is my belief, and it is quite beyond me to verify it so as to destroy all reasonable alternatives to it.

Nor is a religious experience a fact except to the person who has had it. All my life I have been around Middle-Class Christians who testify that through a direct encounter with Christ their lives have been radically changed. Most of them witness to this experience, telling others the story. Such a witness is in good New Testament tradition, beginning with the disciples. The experience is a very real fact for them. It happened to them.

But your religious experience is nontransferable. It occurred in the context of your personality, your needs, and your personal history, none of which are duplicated in any other human being. It is authentic for you, but it is not authentic for anyone else. It does not measure up to the definition of fact.

I have to admit that for a long time I wasn't too finicky about facts. My memory can't quite resurrect the point at which I said to myself, "Let's take a closer look at these contentions which my inherited faith claims to be true." But a fair guess would be that it occurred when some alert layman in one of my early congregations challenged something I had said in a sermon. If so, I offer a belated appreciation to this unknown Christian soldier who nailed me for some unsupported assertion about the faith. He generated in me a process which, if at times productive of discomfort and even trauma, has been ultimately so much more satisfying than an easy and credulous acceptance of every item in the faith I had received.

I soon found out that it isn't as easy to handle faith

questions honestly as I had thought it would be. For one thing, not all the MCCs in my congregations appreciated my efforts to deal honestly with faith questions. They assumed the absolute accuracy of the particular version of the faith they had inherited and therefore looked on any questions I raised about it or deviation from it as an attack on truth itself. How refreshing it was to discover that the agnostics and detractors of the faith, even the learned ones, simply reversed the attitude of the uncritical pious and assumed that nothing in the faith could possibly be accurate or true!

Even feeble attempts at honest handling of faith questions can create hostility within the Christian establishment—and I was part of the establishment. I recall vividly when I was first jolted with the information that the Christian establishment, my brand anyway, did not necessarily welcome open and honest questions.

I was a freshly minted ordinand serving my first full-time parish when the entire denomination was organized for what was called a campaign of personal evangelism. Emissaries from our equivalent of the Vatican were shot out like pellets from a shotgun to every area of the country to tell the clergy how to get on with the job. It was explained that what we were after was individual "commitments to Christ," and that this was to be accomplished by persuading people to sign a card that they committed themselves to Christ and also promised to join our particular church.

Well, full of idealism, hubris, and maybe some intellectual pride, I got up and said that to equate Christian commitment with a signature on a card, obtained much as an insurance salesman would get a signature on a contract, seemed to me a dishonest use of language and a chintzy way to go about anything as serious as a faith decision. Perhaps, in my innocence, I expected an open and

30

lively discussion of the ideas I had injected into the meeting. What I got was cold hostility from the organization man out of denominational headquarters. The guy sloughed me off and took up the problem of always having at least two sharpened pencils on you in case the prospect broke the point of one and changed his mind about signing before you could find another. I also received a subsequent warning from my bishop that troublemakers had dim prospects for advancement in our denomination.

It is possible that I put my point undiplomatically. But I was posing a valid question, and the religious establishment should have dealt with it honestly. Religious establishments are hardly ever willing to deal with faith questions honestly, I'm afraid, and this is why there is a growing disenchantment with organized Christianity today.

To handle your faith questions honestly you have to want to be honest. Not everyone wants to be honest with his faith. Some people are naturally credulous. They find it easy to believe and apparently make no distinction between what is reasonable to believe and what is preposterous. Others have a powerful need to believe, a need we all share. But for some the need is so intense that it squelches all questions or doubts. Still others derive their faith-knowledge and assurance through mystical experience which for them abrogates the inclination to rely on facts, logic, reason, or any source of information outside themselves.

And there are those—many of them—who feel personally inadequate to cope with faith questions or are disinclined to come to grips with them. So they surrender their privilege to query their faith to the pope or some other authority figure in whom they have confidence.

If you fall into one of the above categories, then being honest in the way you handle your faith is not a consideration for you. Not that you want to be dishonest. But

31

if you are credulous, or have to believe something in spite of evidence, or have knowledge through mystical experience, or accept as incontestable some authority, then there is no room for questions so far as you are concerned.

Most of us who have been brought up as Middle-Class Christians have a bit of each of these categories in us. A certain quotient of credulity is mixed up with a need to believe in most of us. Fewer, perhaps, depend on mystical experience, but the average MCC is brought up to believe in the presence of Christ in his life and to depend on the guidance of the Holy Spirit. And all of us have our religious authority figures—John Wesley, or Martin Luther, or John Calvin, or the pope, or Billy Graham, or someone.

I know I have all these elements in me. I have already spoken of my belief bias in favor of the Christian faith. I'm a little wary of mystical experience, probably because of the grotesque varieties of it that I have been exposed to, but I am not prepared to deny the authenticity of all mystical experience. And I think John Wesley is a sound authority some of the time, and Martin Luther a lot of the time.

But somewhere along the way I began to depend on two additional checks—reason and personal experience. Finally, it seemed to me, my faith had to make sense and had to be consistent with my experience in the world or I had a credibility gap.

Chapter Three

EVEN IF
IT'S REASONABLE
IT'S STILL
FAITH

EARLY ON IN MY EXAMINATION of my inherited faith I discovered that Middle-Class Christianity has a peculiarly ambivalent attitude toward the function of man's powers of reason. Reason is treated like a queen in every area of secular endeavor. Does this business deal have a reasonable chance to succeed? Does it make better sense to build a new home or buy one? What is the most profitable use of that piece of land I own? What are the pros and cons of buying mutual funds? No businessman would think of launching a new enterprise without carefully weighing the facts and figures.

But when it comes to his faith, the MCC demotes reason from her queenly throne and views her as a lady of uncertain virtue likely to seduce him from the pure religion to which he intends to remain loyal.

My early college years were spent in an institution more noted for its conservative theological character than for the quality of its education. Evangelists came by in a perpetual parade to exhort us. Many of the professors were ex-missionaries or preachers who found the classroom more congenial than the parish. Doses of theology accompanied the lectures in most of the academic disciplines. So primary was religion in the school's scale of values that cynical students (and some of the pious, too) often managed to evade class sessions for which they were unprepared, or even postponed examinations by generating a discussion of some religious topic, initiating a period of personal testimony, or, as a last resort, igniting a season of prayer. It was at this time in my life that I first became aware of the low esteem in which reason was held by Middle-Class Christians. Not only was it graded F as an aid to piety but was actually pointed to as an insidious enemy of true religious faith and devotion. The life of faith was lived by revelation, we were told, and reason was vastly inferior to revelation as a source of faith and knowledge. Reason was an acid which attacked and macerated the fibers of spiritual certainty.

This attitude bothered me. Although at the time I was insufficiently schooled in the disciplines of theology and logic to formulate my objections concisely, they probably could have been articulated something like this: If the doctrine of creation is true, as every orthodox Christian since the Gnostic heresy has claimed, then how can a man of faith look on human reason, which is a part of God's creation and one of God's great gifts, as an enemy of the spiritual life?

A subsequent thirty years as a parish pastor demonstrated to me that discounting the role of reason in matters of faith was not a franchise held only by Christians of a conservative theological persuasion. All Middle-Class Christians do it. And they do it because they rely on the deductive method of reasoning.

Deductive reasoning is when you start with a theory, or a philosophy, or a theology, or a faith which you assume is true and accurate. From this total view, then, you examine all facts, truths, phenomena, ideas, or whatever so as to harmonize them with it.

Even If It's Reasonable It's Still Faith

I bumped up against an instance of deductive reasoning on the part of an MCC quite recently—a lady, about forty, bright, vivacious, obviously possessed of a high intelligence, a graduate in biology from a major university. In our conversation she said that as a biology major she was familiar with the theory and evidence for biological evolution. The evidence was strong, she said, and from a scientific point of view powerfully supportive of the theory of evolution. But, she added, of course the theory was in error.

I asked her why she said this. Because, she replied, the creation story in Genesis was God's literal account of what really happened, so it had to be accurate. Therefore any theory, no matter if it is buttressed by impressive scientific evidence, has to be false if it in any way contravenes the Genesis account.

This is deductive reasoning.

The lady lives in the modern world. She is a typical Middle-Class Christian, except maybe she is above average in affluence and education. Her personal spiritual history, though, is typical. She inherited her faith. She nourishes it in a fellowship of like-minded Christians. She begins with what is for her an unassailable set of truths. If facts come along indicating that her unassailable truths won't hold water, then the facts must be rejected because they have to be wrong.

Rather early I began to go about finding my faith positions by a different route. I began to follow the inductive method of reasoning, even before I knew that was what it is called. Inductive reasoning begins with the parts rather than the whole. Instead of saying, "This I believe. Now let's organize the facts in the light of my faith," you say, "Let's look at the facts and see what it is reasonable to believe."

Perhaps history's best-known instance of the clash between the deductive method and the inductive method of reasoning is Galileo's discovery that the planets revolve around the sun. The Christian establishment of the time rejected Galileo's findings. "It is Christian dogma," the establishment said, "that the earth is the center of the universe. Therefore, everything in the universe must revolve about the earth."

Galileo replied, "But take a look at my evidence, and you will see beyond a reasonable doubt that the earth revolves around the sun."

The church answered, "It is unnecessary to look at your evidence because we know that what you say the evidence indicates couldn't possibly be true." Then it added, "And by the way, Galileo, you had better shut up about this or it will be too bad for you."

Perhaps I am biased in favor of the inductive method because history shows me that the people who have adhered stoutly to the deductive method have an impressive record of being wrong. Calvin in his controversy with Servetus, for example. Or the Roman church versus Luther on the validity of papal infallibility. Or the solid citizens of Salem, Massachusetts, burning a number of ladies on the assumption that they were witches.

At any rate, I am convinced that the Middle-Class Christian penchant for resorting to the deductive method in matters of faith is to be deplored. It can lead you to all sorts of spiritual destinations where you hadn't ought to be.

Now I am not claiming that man can only live by provable propositions. The most faithful follower of the inductive method finally puts the various parts of his evidence together into an hypothesis which is his speculation as to what the evidence indicates.

For example: As I began to question my inherited faith, the central question for me was, Does God exist? Professional theologians might say that this isn't where we ought to begin, but my own experience plus decades of dealing with the faith problems of my parishioners convinces me that this is *the* question which is always lurking in the mind of the Middle-Class Christian, the man in the pew who is depending on his faith to get him through the daily combat with the world, the flesh, and the devil. Never mind the theological nuances of the nature of God, or the concept of existence, or even how God is supposed to operate in the world. Is he there?

If the answer to that is no, then the MCC is playing by the wrong rules. If the answer is no, then it's another kind of ball game. There are plenty of other questions the MCC is interested in asking, but they are all pendant to the central question. You can't even ask them unless the answer to the central question is yes.

A lady of mature years and widely known for her devotion to faith and church once said to me, "If I didn't believe that God exists and that he rewards me for being good and punishes me for being bad, then I would see no point in being good."

Most of us might not be so candid about it, or would phrase it differently, but that's it for us Middle-Class Christians. God exists and operates in the world and with people in knowable ways, and we put our lives together around this proposition. If he doesn't exist, then the reason we believe what we believe, the basis for our values, the foundation for our ethics, and the rationale for our behavior all disappear. Some people argue that it is possible or even desirable to build a faith and choose values and create an ethic if the answer to our central question is no. But we don't see it that way. We're betting our whole bundle that the answer to the central question is yes.

Incidentally, though alluding to the life of faith by the gambling metaphor may appear to some as impious or blasphemous, it isn't. Preachers and theologians, all with pious credentials in good order, have been doing this for a long time. I remember as a boy hearing pulpiteers of spotless evangelical loyalty and who, I feel certain, would have been unable to define daily double or comprehend the perils of drawing to an inside straight, describe Christian commitment as "betting your life on God." The metaphor appealed to me then, and it still does. Offhand, I can't think of a more precise and succinct device for profiling what religious faith, or at least the kind of religious faith I inherited, is all about.

But is it a good bet? Why should I lay my money on the proposition "God exists"?

The Bible tells me God exists.

Jesus bet everything he had on it.

My inherited faith taught me to bank on it.

My parents, my grandparents believed it, and probably as far back as my antecedents are traceable it was assumed to be true, so my family tradition affirms it.

My culture, my country, the whole Western world is more or less rooted in the proposition "God exists." And while the atheist or the agnostic doesn't excite antagonism or risk ostracism as he once did, he is still dismissed as a kook, a person who bears watching, as politically unreliable, or at best as a benighted intellectual (intellectual being used as an opprobrious label).

So almost everything in the life of a Middle-Class Christian like me urges, exhorts, presses me to bet yes on the proposition "God exists."

But Jimmy the Greek, the celebrated Las Vegas odds maker who rates the probable outcome of everything from elections to horse races, wouldn't consider this proposition anywhere near a sure thing. He would put me in the same category as the guy who picks a horse because some race-track tout told him the horse was bound to win.

Even If It's Reasonable It's Still Faith

It finally came to me, as I thrashed my way through the thicket of faith questions, that none of the reasons supporting my belief in the existence of God met the requirements of facts.

I can insist that the Bible couldn't be wrong, but that is a belief and not a fact.

I can claim that Jesus is a sure and certain authority, but how do I know?

I can say that I have a powerful inner conviction that God is there, or that I have direct communion with him, but what does that prove?

It proves that I have a strong need or desire to make it come out that the answer is yes. It indicates my pro-God bias.

I recognized that I had a pro-God bias (and still have, of course). But I also recognized that the bias was marshy footing for a faith. I felt that the answer had to be yes, but I also saw that to come within waving distance of honesty I had to admit the possibility that the answer was no. When you admit the possibility that the answer is no, you resort to the inductive method of reasoning—or at least that is when I did.

You don't have to be a trained theologian to ruminate on the bits and pieces of information available which can help you decide whether the probable answer to the question "Does God exist?" is yes or no. This isn't a treatise on systematic theology, which I couldn't write even if I wanted to, so we won't drag through all the classic arguments for the existence of God. Let's look at one, though, which is persuasive for many, maybe most people.

We observe our environment, the world we live in. It apparently functions in a reliable fashion. Light travels at a constant speed. The rather complex conditions capable of sustaining life are present in it. It is not unreasonable to call it a purposive mechanism. What does the nature of my environment suggest to me?

Let's be honest and admit that it may say nothing but that the planet earth just by accident of nature happened to combine all the necessities for life. It could be that there is no significance in it at all. This is one explanation, and quite a few intelligent people subscribe to it.

Or, I can speculate on my observations and conclude something like this: "My environment apparently fulfills the definition of a coordinated mechanism. The only kind of a coordinated system, device, or machine I know anything about existed first in the mind of its creator. Anything I know which was created for a purpose implies a purposer behind it. It is therefore reasonable for me to infer that this world, this universe, existed first in the mind of one who brought it into being by a creative act. The name we give to this creative mind is God."

My reasoning here is a sort of sketchy version of what philosophers and theologians call the teleological argument for the existence of God. What I have done is to take an observation, seek an explanation for it, and formulate an hypothesis which states my explanation. I have to be careful not to make excessive claims for my hypothesis. We Middle-Class Christians, with our pro-God bias, almost always are guilty of overclaim when it comes to evidence for the existence of God. My hypothesis is not proof. It is only one reasonable explanation. There are reasonable alternative explanations, and I am dishonest if I don't admit it. Personally, I don't worry much about absolute, incontrovertible proof that the answer to our question about God's existence is yes. I don't worry about it because this side of the Second Coming no such proof will be forthcoming.

A student once said to the late Paul Tillich, a great theologian, "Prove to me that God exists, and then I'll be a believer." Tillich said to him, "What would be proof?"

Tillich's point was that no proof will be forthcoming. But the alternative is not an irrational and credulous faith. There is evidence to support a yes answer. There are indications we can trust. An hypothesis is nothing more than a faith that this is how things are. But an hypothesis is not a faith founded on a wild surmise. It is, rather, rooted in a reasonable interpretation of evidence. As Nero Wolfe once said to a worried client, "It is wise to reject all suppositions . . . until surmise can stand on the legs of fact."

So it shakes out that the gambling metaphor holds good. As the evangelists are fond of saying, being a Christian is betting your life on God. But it doesn't have to be a stupid bet or an uninformed bet. I'm not going to lay it all on the line if I think the odds aren't favorable, and I doubt if you are either when you stop to think about it. It's dumb to bet your life on God unless there is some impressive evidence that you are onto a good thing.

Damon Runyon once made a remark about gambling which applies to one's choice of faith too. "The race may not always be to the swift," he said, "nor the battle to the strong—but that's the way to bet."

That's the way to bet.

Chapter Four

IS
GOD GOOD
FOR
ANYTHING?

IN MY MIDDLE-CLASS CHRISTIAN circles we not only had our bets down on God, we also spoke of him with affection and partisan bias, much as the more passionate supporters of Notre Dame laud skills and virtues of their team apparent to the faithful but hidden from more detached observers.

Our concept of God was not so crass as critics of Middle-Class Christianity like to make out that it was and is. I don't know any MCCs who think of God as the man upstairs or as a celestial Santa Claus although there may be some. We anthropomorphized God, of course, meaning that our imaginations (with assists from preachers and Sunday school teachers) clothed the bones of God as pure spirit with the flesh of human personality. Nothing wrong with that. How else can you envision pure spirit? And isn't that what the incarnation was all about?

We believed that God is love, that he is the father of our Lord Jesus Christ, and all the other theologically correct descriptions of the deity. But we didn't believe these formulas passionately. We loved to sing "God in three persons, blessed Trinity," probably because it has a majestic-sounding tune. But I have yet to meet a Christian layman who can give a coherent explanation of the doctrine of the Trinity, although there must be laymen who can do this.

A recent survey reveals the attitudes of Protestant Christians in the United States and Canada, which is to say the attitudes of American Middle-Class Christians. Overwhelmingly these MCCs voted for the Apostles' Creed as the definitive statement of faith they prefer and stated that they want no one tampering with it, updating it, or reinterpreting it. Based on my own experience as a veteran MCC I could have guessed that the survey would have shown such an attitude. Our faith was nourished (if that is the word) on the creed every Sunday. It was a fixed item in our culture. The Apostles' Creed is to Middle-Class Christendom as the Constitution is to the U.S.A. —accepted and honored but not very well understood. I do not doubt that most MCCs believe they believe the Apostles' Creed, but I do doubt that their affirmation of it affects their lives very much one way or another, and some of it they don't actually believe at all.

What we did believe in as I grew up in Middle-Class Christian culture, believed in with genuine gut conviction, was a God who was good for something. It didn't really make any difference to us, much as we approved of it, that God is composed of three persons somehow combined in one person. But a God who serves as a buffer against the unpleasant uncertainties of an unpredictable world, a God who guarantees that what you care about— your country, your society, your values, whatever—is what you ought to care about, well, that's a God worth having, that's a useful sort of God, a God who is good for something.

In some ways the toughest match in my wrestlings with my inherited faith was this battle to make sense out of the idea of God bequeathed to me by my Middle-Class Christianity. "God Will Take Care of You," "Leaning on the Everlasting Arms," "Rock of Ages," and other hymnodic assurances that so long as I passed inspection I would be exempt from the unlovely experiences reserved for the wicked pelted me every Sunday. The point of most of the preaching to which I was exposed was that if I were in the will of God life would work out for me in rewarding ways. The corollary of this point was that people outside the divine intention could expect to catch life's haymakers in the solar plexus.

I don't remember much about the process of rethinking the MCC idea of God. Not many people suddenly say, "Hey, I'm going to change my mind about what God is like." At least I didn't. We don't discard the items of our spiritual heritage easily. They are like family heirlooms—circumstances may force us to part with them, but we do so reluctantly and one by one. Probably there were many influences combining to force the reevaluation.

But dragging the bottom of my memory does dredge up one vivid picture. Decades of dealing with MCCs had shown me that lurking beneath the surface of the typical Middle-Class Christian's standard affirmations about God was the conviction that God would do a lot for him if he could make a favorable impression on God. We all ask the question, ask it below the level of conscious expression, because it would be crude and irreverent to phrase it, If I serve God, what's in it for me?

I never sat down and made a list of questions to ponder or extracted the elements in the MCC concept of God for analysis, but if I had, it would have been something like this: Our creeds state that God is the father of us all, but we seem to believe that God prefers American middle-class cultural values above all others, that God believes in our free-enterprise economic system, that God supports without fail the military endeavors of the United States, and that God isn't quite as keen on the colored races as he is on the white.

Put this way it sounds like a caricature of Middle-Class Christian faith. I do not think that it is. I feel certain it is a fair representation of what American Middle-Class Christians actually believe as opposed to what they say they believe.

I think it is accurate because whenever I preached a sermon that suggested any of the tenets of our actual faith were false (for example, that God does not automatically support the United States in any conflict with communism) I always provoked a blizzard of angry objections.

I think it is accurate because these are the things that I, who pretend to openmindedness, tend to believe despite my intellectual rejection of each item. I've been exposed to some other cultures, and I still like mine the best. I've been in Communist countries, and, from what I could observe, I can't imagine why anyone who had a choice would prefer communism over our free-enterprise system, flawed as it is. I don't like any military endeavor, but when my country is in one, I'd hope it could get out without taking a thrashing. I have sound liberal attitudes on the race question, but I'm glad I'm not yellow or red or black or even brown (except when the brown is acquired by lying on a beach somewhere and I know no one will mistake it for my true pigmentation).

Does God play favorites? Most MCCs would answer no, but we really believe that the Almighty is manipulable. We really believe that he can be cajoled. We seek to cajole him by our repentance or our subscription to certain dogmas or obedience to the Decalogue or by undergoing a spiritual experience or by striking accredited pious stances. We attempt to manipulate him by loyalty to a religious institution or by tithing our income or by performing good works or by devotional practices or by a combination of these. We expect this cajolery to bring us material prosperity or good health or peace of mind and ultimately, of course, admission to heaven.

Somewhere along the line I began to wonder what was the essential difference between the God of Middle-Class Christianity and a tribal deity of the sort we find in the fiercer parts of the Old Testament, and I had to conclude that there isn't much difference. Admitting this, it was easy to see that we had gone about the business of discovering what God is like exactly backward. Instead of looking for evidence exterior to us, we consulted our own insides and decided what we wanted in a god. It's something like selecting the options on that dandy Detroit deluxe model you ordered. It's as if you started with the austerity model god, basic god, and chose to add the special interior trim and decorative wheel covers and automatic transmission and power-assisted windows and a multitude of desirable extras until you have what amounts to a god customized to your needs and tastes.

The Bible's name for buying a god manufactured to your own specifications is idolatry. This practice has been going on a long time, and preachers and prophets and theologians keep telling us it is still going on, but I can't see that they have made much of a dent in us. The trouble with idolatry is that it seems like such a good idea at the time.

Anyway, my discovery that I was an idolater had serious side effects for me. For one thing, I had to quit beginning sentences with "God wants you to . . ." or "God demands that you . . ." or "God expects you to . . ." because, reflection showed, the rest of these sentences always ended up as an affirmation of some idolatrous proposition. Now, whenever someone says to me (either from the pulpit or in conversation), "God wants you to do this or that," I tune him out because I am pretty sure he is going to tell me what he wants, or what the religious institution wants, or what the congregation wants to hear, and blame it on God. I may miss some theological edification or the illumination of eternal verities by shutting out the rest of the sentence, but I'll just have to chance it.

Then, I had to erase my inherited ideas about God and begin all over again. That's painful. I'm convinced, though, that until Middle-Class Christians begin all over again with the idea of God, the health that is in middle-class Christendom will continue to leak out of it. The history of religion tells us that if your God is no more than a tribal deity, an idol (even a highly polished, attractive, and eminently satisfactory idol), one of these days a stronger tribe will kick your god out and install its god. You might not believe this, but it always happens.

I can claim no extraordinary erudition, and I'm only a journeyman theologian. No special revelation has zinged around me in lightning from above, nor have the heavens rolled back to afford me a glimpse of what others cannot see. My conclusions carry no imprimatur of authority. I'm a Middle-Class Christian, just like you, except that maybe I have hacked my way through this jungle ahead of you, and if I tell you what I have found there, it might be useful to you as you try to find your way. Thus qualified, then, here are some of the products of my cogitations, of my beginning again with the idea of God.

We ought to abandon the quick-draw habit when using the name of God. By this I mean we MCCs pull out the name *God* too quickly, too easily, and too often whenever it suits our purposes. For example, you can tell me that I ought to support a return to prohibition because alcohol is a highway killer and alcoholism a life-wrecking disease, but don't tell me I ought to support it because

The Case of a Middle-Class Christian

God wants me to. God may or may not want me to support a return to prohibition. I don't know—and neither do you. All you know for certain is that you want me to support it, and to attribute your personal convictions to God comes pretty close to blasphemy and is for sure idolatry.

Then, I concluded, there are only three sources of information for what God is like. They are: creation, authority, and personal experience. All three sources, it seemed to me, have something to tell us about what God is like, but they are not equally reliable. This is because only creation is external to us. We didn't dream up the universe. And how other people behave has nothing to do with our inner feelings. Conclusion: What I learn about the Creator from observing his creation—the universe and what is in it, including us—is likely to be more reliable than what I learn from authority and from personal experience, either my own or the experiences reported by other people. It isn't always easy to interpret correctly my observations of the universe, of course. Even highly trained scientists often argue about this. But when I do interpret these observations correctly, the information about God this yields me is reliable.

This does not mean that authority (the pope, a church, official dogma) is necessarily wrong or that it is never helpful in telling us about God. But we have to remember that authority is often a tainted source of information.

Having spent many years as a part of an ecclesiastical organization, I have to admit that ecclesiastical authority always has reasons other than a passion for truth for wanting you to believe what it says is true. Nothing in the nature of God, as described to us by ecclesiastical authority, is ever a threat to the ecclesiastical organization. That should be enough to make us just a little suspicious.

Is God Good for Anything?

Information about God which I get from religious authority is also slightly suspect because I choose my authority from among many possible religious authorities. As a Middle-Class Protestant Christian I accept the Bible as the ultimate religious authority. But is the Bible a better source of information about God than the Koran? I think so, but my Mohammedan brother would think not. He chooses the Koran. I am a United Methodist. But are the pronouncements of United Methodist councils and theologians as to the nature of the Deity more enlightening than the writings of Mary Baker Eddy? I choose to believe the information from the United Methodist source is more reliable, but Christian Scientists prefer Mrs. Eddy.

But you don't have to decide about creation. It's there. All you can do is observe it and draw your conclusions. What you think or wish or feel does not affect its operation. You may insist that the sun revolves around the earth, but the earth will go right on revolving around the sun.

The lesson here is that when the observation of creation and the pronouncements of authority conflict in telling us what God is like (and they often do conflict), then creation is our surer source of information.

And depending on personal experience—my own and the experiences of others—as a source of information for what God is like is valuable but not conclusive. Here again, I have to choose in whom I shall believe.

As a Protestant I am favorably disposed toward Martin Luther's thinking and personal experience as a trustworthy source of information about God. As a Methodist I am inclined to listen to what John Wesley had to say on the subject. I give more weight to the experiences of Luther and Wesley than to what the monk Rasputin or the founder of some offbeat sect tells me. But whose experiences of God, whose thinking about God, is authentic and whose isn't is still a choice I make.

Middle-Class Christians tend to pay more attention to information on what God is like when it comes from some authority and from personal experience (more often the reported experiences of others than their own) and less attention when it comes from creation. That's why we so easily become idolaters.

Rather early in my personal history as a Middle-Class Christian I felt a need to know all there was to know about God. I would guess that any MCC who takes his faith at all seriously shares this need. However, I came to realize that the reliable information available to me was scarcer than I wished it to be, and much scarcer than the Niagara of information about God pouring forth from preachers, evangelists, theologians, churches, sects, and even from movie stars and professional athletes. I reflected, and I think soundly, that a god who can be precisely described—how he talks to me, how he responds to me, how he rewards me, how he punishes me, and so on—is more likely to be an idol than the one true God.

Conclusion: I prefer a Divine Mystery, God as ultimately unfathomable, to a god reduced to my size, a god who can be measured and fully described and put to work for my personal benefit.

Can God be manipulated? Will he, under certain circumstances, do favors for me? If I serve him loyally, is there something in it for me?

If you answer yes, yes, yes, then you aren't looking for "God the Father Almighty, maker of heaven and earth," but for a power which you can tap and wire into your own purposes. And that's idolatry.

Is God good for anything? The answer has to be no if by good for anything you mean God can be employed to your advantage.

Is God Good for Anything?

Middle-Class Christians find it nigh impossible to give up their idea of a God who is going to do good things for them. But the sun still shines on the just and the unjust, and a tribal deity is still a tribal deity even if it is our tribe that serves it. I didn't like giving up the god who is especially partial to Middle-Class Christianity, and you won't like it either. But you have to give it up or be an idolater. You have no other choice.

Chapter Five

THE NEED
TO KNOW MORE
ABOUT
JESUS

I DID NOT FIND IT EASY to reinspect my inherited Middle-Class Christian concept of God, and discovering that I had been an idolater jarred me some. It was a temptation to stop at God. Spiritual fatigue sets in, and you think maybe you have had enough of this reexamining-your-faith business. But you realize you can't quit now. We also have inherited an MCC Jesus Christ. Maybe he reflects the New Testament portrait of Jesus, and maybe he doesn't. You won't be happy until you have checked it out.

Middle-Class Christian kids are brought up on Jesus. The flaking brown walls of gloomy Sunday school class-rooms are hung with talentless drawings of Jesus as a sweet little shepherd boy. Lay teachers dragooned into service stumble through denominational lessons in an attempt to squirt some information about Jesus into the minds of disinterested church-school pupils. We learned the Lord's Prayer by rote. We heard the name of Jesus constantly in hymn and prayer and in the patois of the pious.

I have tried to reconstruct what I, as a Middle-Class

Christian child, learned about Jesus. It was something like this:

1. He was a nice little boy.

2. He grew up to be a nice young man who had magical powers and tried to persuade people to be good.

3. Some bad people hung him on a cross, and he died, but God didn't want him to die, so he brought him back to life.

4. I am supposed to try to be like Jesus. This means being good and not causing anybody any trouble.

As you grow up, you graduate to Jesus the mystical savior. And if you hang in there, as I did, you finally deal with the Incarnation, the dual nature of Christ, the creedal descriptions, Jesus' sinless humanity, and · the Second Coming.

If I recall accurately my reaction to these three stages of learning about Jesus Christ, they were: to the childhood teachings, indifference or at best a very mild interest; to Christ the mystical savior, inability to grasp the concept; and to the creedal descriptions, complete confusion.

That I went ahead to study theology and become a practitioner of the Christian ministry was in spite of and not because of my Middle-Class Christian teachings about Jesus. Subsequent experience has convinced me that most MCCs react to their Christian education about as I did, which is to say that the Middle-Class Christian Christ is not a compelling force in their lives. The Jesus of their childhood is too simplistic to be taken seriously, and the Christ of the creeds is too confusing to seem real.

As a child attending Sunday school, I cast God in the lead part on the movie screen of my imagination, with Jesus in a small supporting role. God was the guy who dealt out reward or punishment according to a merit system supposedly fashioned on Sinai but actually constructed by parents, church, and elders of the community to fit their need for keeping kids in line.

God was very real to me because he was a factor in my life. The Jesus taught to me in Sunday school, which I now know was almost totally a work of fiction, couldn't have been taken seriously by any normal youngster because that kind of Jesus didn't matter one way or another. A sweet little boy who was always good didn't grab us. The only little boys we knew who were always good were mother-dominated and lacked the imagination and animal spirits to test the limits of parentally prescribed behavior. You just can't respect a kid like that.

But as you mature, if you stick with the faith, the situation reverses itself. God recedes as a reality and Jesus becomes more and more central. At some point along the way thoughtful adults realize that Jesus is *the* reality with which Christians have to come to terms.

I have often wished that there was some way for me to have a fresh look at Jesus, a new view uncontaminated by half a century of teaching, propaganda, theological indoctrination, and pious attitudes. But you cannot wipe your memory clean. There is no records shredder for the mind which can make confetti of all those mingled facts and fictions. Not for Middle-Class Christians. Not for me. Too much has been etched into our memories for it to be expunged. But I decided to try anyway.

I devised a game of imagining that I had never heard of Jesus. Then I read the Gospels as if this were my first acquaintance with them. Imperfect as the exercise may have been, given my lengthy marination in Jesus information and theologies and Christologies, I was compelled to conclude that this was the only logical way to begin.

Even though the four Gospels—Matthew, Mark, Luke, and John—are the only sources we have for information about Jesus, most Middle-Class Christians haven't read one of them for years, if indeed they ever did. The average MCC relies on someone else—a preacher, a teacher, a religious-minded friend—for information about Jesus. I was a mature adult, an ordained clergyman yet, before it sunk in on me that I was practicing and even preaching a secondhand religion. What I thought and felt and believed about Jesus was what someone else had told me I ought to think and feel and believe. I had read the Gospels, of course, but mostly for the purpose of confirming what I had already been told I would find there.

But back to our game. The following rules are nonnegotiable:

1. You have no previous knowledge or concept of Jesus Christ.

2. You cannot assume, for the duration of the game, that the Bible is anything more than an ancient collection of books.

3. Since you don't know anything about Jesus, there is no such thing as an heretical idea or interpretation of him.

4. You are going to try to evaluate the information about Jesus as you would evaluate information about George Washington or King Henry VIII—that is, you are going to try to be objective.

So, what do I find when I look into the Gospels? As to Jesus' profile I find that he was born to a Middle Eastern Jewish peasant family, and probably was taught carpentry, his father's trade. Sometime around his thirtieth year he was baptized by a preacher of repentance and righteousness named John, who was apparently Jesus' cousin. After his baptism he became an itinerant preacher who was reported to have worked many miracles, mostly healing the sick. He claimed his power and authority flowed from God. He formed a movement of sorts by gathering round him twelve constant companions and an undetermined number of supporters and friends. He was highly critical of the Jewish religious establishment, which saw Jesus as a threat to its security. The religious establishment persuaded the Roman provincial governor to condemn Jesus as an insurrectionist and execute him by crucifixion. He was placed in a tomb owned by one of his wealthy followers, but, according to accounts of his disciples, God raised him from the dead after three days. He was reported to have been seen by his disciples and followers in Galilee.

There is more, though. For my purposes, I felt it necessary to look for two things: what Jesus said and what Jesus was. As to what Jesus said, I found that his biographers had reported rather fully. There is enough material to give us the shape of his mind, the thrust of his message. From what he said I was able to distill the essentials of his message. These, it seemed to me, were:

(a) Jesus' main concern, by far, was to tell us what is the nature and character of God. God is not defined as a righteous judge pronouncing sentence on those who break the law and passing out rewards to those who please him. God is much more like the father in the Parable of the Prodigal Son—he loves the sinner as well as the upright, and he is more than just and even-handed—he is merciful and forgiving. If we can be certain of only one thing that Jesus taught, this would be it.

(b) Jesus believed that self-respect coupled with a concern for other people is our proper response to God's merciful attitude toward us.

(c) The world is God's gift to us. It is good. We are to respect it, use it wisely, and enjoy it.

(d) The Kingdom of God will be accomplished only in the future, and when God decides. But it is also here now and can be entered and enjoyed by anyone who responds to God as indicated in (b) and (c).

56

Jesus said much more than this, of course, but for the purposes of simplicity this sums it up.

In general the Gospels describe a man who was quite unlike the nice young man of Sunday school art and literature. Jesus must have been a magnetic personality, a man of vigorous nature with strong personal convictions. He was intimately acquainted with the traditions and Scriptures of the Jewish religion and thought of himself as a Jew, but brought fresh interpretations and insights to his inherited faith.

His biographers claim that Jesus was the son of God, although they do not tell us what they meant by that phrase. Jesus himself never claimed that he was the son of God, or, if he did, his biographers did not record it. They do record that Jesus had a reputation for liking dinner parties, and we know from experience that grim types who never crack a smile neither enjoy parties nor get invited to them very often.

The Gospels tell us nothing of the texture of Jesus' life with his family and community. Was Jesus married? We wish the Gospel writers had told us if he had been because today some people say there is evidence that he was married. Others say he was celibate. Yet others "prove" that he was homosexual or that he had a heterosexual relationship (probably with Mary Magdalene). His sexual history had to be one of these four alternatives, but the Gospels are silent about which one it was.

You must admit, the foregoing character sketch does not give one much factual material. I found myself wanting a more fully rounded picture of the kind of person Jesus was than the Gospel glimpses afforded me. What I decided to do was to use my imagination. I would look for clues in the little side events of Jesus' life, the overtones of the Gospel stories which would show me how he reacted in the various small situations with which he had to deal. It is quite clear from the Gospels how he responded to the crucial events of his life—the confrontations with the scribes and Pharisees, the questionings of Pontius Pilate, the crucifixion. But that renders me a one-dimensional picture. I needed more.

To give you an idea how I went about this task, let's consider John's account of the miracle at Cana. A synopsis would read something like this:

Jesus is attending the wedding of an obscure couple at the little village of Cana. The wine runs out. Jesus, notified of the shortage, performs a miracle and turns one hundred twenty gallons of water into one hundred twenty gallons of top-quality wine (it must have been a big party, or its guests persons of impressive capacities).

That's about all there is to the story, but from the Gospel material we can infer a number of details. The couple at Cana obviously had no social standing because John doesn't even bother to name them. They must have been dirt-poor, inasmuch as the groom hadn't been able to lay in enough wine for the wedding reception. Yet Jesus was there. This tells me something about his values. Friends were friends to him without any reference to their social and economic status. How odd that the Messiah would waste his precious time at a grubby little wedding of nobodies. But he was there.

Furthermore, we would think that a miracle is merited only for some high and noble purpose. What is the point of providing more wine for people who have probably already had more than is good for them? And was it necessary to turn the water into vintage grade rather than the ordinary stuff the guests had been drinking?

What comes through to us here is that Jesus was a man who valued personal relationships no matter how humble and that he was glad to help a poor young bridegroom save the occasion of his wedding party. By utilizing the overtones of the story you have the material with which to build a reasonable characterization of Jesus.

Another example. Matthew, in the twenty-sixth chapter of his Gospel, tells the story of a nameless woman who came up to Jesus and poured a jar of very expensive ointment on his head. The disciples reacted with a disgruntled practicality. What a stupid waste, they said. This foolish woman could have sold that ointment for a bundle, given the proceeds to us, and we could have administered it for the benefit of the poor. Jesus came down on them hard. You will always have the poor, but you won't always have me. She has anointed me in preparation for my death. She has done a beautiful thing, so don't fuss at her.

Bible commentaries say that Matthew's purpose in telling the story is to preenact Jesus' death, and to show how dense the disciples were. They just didn't understand all that Jesus had been telling them.

The overtones of the story, which Matthew probably didn't even think of, are: Jesus takes what we might consider a callous attitude toward the poor, and we could infer that he is a harsh man—except that he has demonstrated over and over his concern for the unfortunate of this world. I am chagrined to admit that I would have reacted about as the disciples reacted, and I'll bet most MCCs would be on the side of the disciples in this one. We are brought up to have a horror of waste. We are taught to be practical in all things. The very thought of pouring away several hundred dollars appalls us. But Jesus says the woman has done "a beautiful thing" and commends her in extravagant language. Jesus demonstrates by his approval of the woman's act that life, rightly lived, needs a balance of beauty and the practical. Life can't be all one color, one dimension. The wise man knows when to give precedence to one over the other.

The Case of a Middle-Class Christian

I am sure that my overtone method of exegesis would shock competent New Testament scholars. I submit it without defense except that in searching for what Jesus means to me I had to resort to it. I can confess that Jesus is Lord of life, the Lamb of God, the Messiah. But these are abstractions, remote and even a little forbidding. We are taught to affirm Jesus by these designations, but they never were very real to me, and I doubt if they grab the imaginations of most MCCs.

The Jesus that does seem real to me is the Jesus who had the secret of what human life is all about, who—in the somewhat slangy description coined by one of my friends—"got it all together."

A person with no previous knowledge of Jesus would probably be puzzled if he observed how most Middle-Class Christians react to the Jesus he had read about in the Gospels. He would wonder why MCCs invoke this radical and nonconforming young man of the Gospels as the sanction for all the careful conformities of MCC culture.

He would read in the Gospels how Jesus challenged the religious authorities but notice that today religious authorities employ Jesus to undergird orthodoxy.

He would read in the Gospels that Jesus had a low opinion of righteousness achieved by following religious prescriptions, but observe that today middle-class Christianity preaches salvation by following rules—and preaches it in Jesus' name.

I respond to the Jesus who broke all the conventions of the middle-class religion of his day and gladly had dinner in the house of Zacchaeus, partly motivated I suppose by the chance of converting a sinner, but also because he thought Zacchaeus—sinner that he was—would be good company (and maybe because Jesus calculated that Zacchaeus set the best table in town).

I can identify with the Jesus whom Luke shows me more

clearly than the other evangelists, the Jesus who is always especially concerned for the disinherited of the world, who sees the good and the admirable in the spiritual outsiders which others did not see (for example, the Good Samaritan).

I believe with 100 percent of myself in Jesus' counsel that we should "take no thought for the morrow." I believe, and I doubt that anything can alter the conviction, that the right way to live is to live a day at a time, realizing the opportunities and potential and pleasures and coping with the pain and frustrations and disappointments of each twenty-four hours as they come.

Now this way of living runs counter to everything in the MCC make-up, tradition, training, and stance toward life.

The Protestant ethic teaches us to postpone today's pleasure and possibilities by the practice of a present frugality—both of the pocketbook and the spirit—for a future security. We strap ourselves to buy life insurance, and if we are lucky enough to make some money, we frantically search for tax shelters, and we even prepay our funeral expenses. And who's to say this isn't sensible? A man's an idiot not to lay up a little something against the future if he can manage it, and even Jesus probably wouldn't condemn some hedge against the hazards of life.

But we MCCs overdo it. You just can't square the over-careful, overcautious, a-penny-saved-is-a-penny-earned life style with "take no thought for the morrow," no matter how you wiggle and squirm.

I know I find it difficult to "take no thought for the morrow." I am, by nature, depressive, pessimistic, and anxiety-ridden. Maybe it's in my genes, or maybe in my diet, or a product of hormonal deficiency, or a failure of faith. I envy the naturally cheerful, and even wish I had been created like such bubbleheads as Mr. Micawber who, in the midst of every possible personal disaster, are optimistic that something good will turn up. An honest appraisal of my life up to now shows that nothing very bad has ever happened to me, but I'm always pretty sure that it will. And I'm afraid that until science invents a booster shot which can change the structure of my personality I'll just have to live with myself as I am.

But there is a very real sense in which Jesus' assurance that life is a good gift, that it should be lived each day joyfully, that I must trust the gift and not fret about it, saves me. In the midst of my frequent blue funks what Jesus said about how I should square away to life (and demonstrated by how he squared away to life) keeps me going. It keeps me from being a total victim of my feelings, and this is at least one definition of salvation.

Where have my attempts to reevaluate my own view of Jesus taken me? To several conclusions:

1. The information about Jesus I had acquired in Sunday school was for the most part false.

2. Middle-Class Christianity, as a rule, doesn't draw its concept of Christ from the Gospels but manufactures a Christ to fit its needs.

3. I am on sounder ground when I start with what the Gospels tell me about Jesus instead of relying on what other people tell me about Jesus.

What I end up with, then, is Jesus as the archetype of humanness. Nothing original about this, of course. It is half of the orthodox Christian description of Jesus as at the same time perfectly divine and perfectly human. And I'm not disposed to argue with those who insist that I have to give equal emphasis to the divine dimension of Jesus Christ. I know all about incarnational theories, and who am I to say they aren't of equal importance with the concept of the Christ who shows me how to be truly human?

I can only say that the divinity of Christ is not as important to me as his humanity.

Conservative Middle-Class Christians will say that I am adopting the classic "moral influence theory" of salvation, and to them "moral influence theory" is a dirty phrase. I claim, of course, that it isn't a disreputable idea, but that's a matter of perspective.

The idea that Jesus saves me by pointing me the way to a true humanness is utterly beyond proof. I can't demonstrate that it is valid. My apprehension of it may be as mystical, if not so dramatic, as St. Paul's experience on the Damascus Road. All I can say for certain is that, for me, it has the clang of reality about it, that I have this gut-feeling that it is right.

And, however inelegant this phrase, it qualifies as a Christian witness.

Chapter Six

DOES ANYONE HERE KNOW HOW TO PLAY THIS GAME?

IF YOU ARE A WITH-IT CHRISTIAN these days, you discuss and speculate on what is the appropriate Christian life style. The secular press breathlessly reports on the doings in Christian communes and the Jesus movement. Even staid church publications abound with solemn examinations of the latest experiments in Christian fashions for living out the faith in the world.

Like all MCCs I was brought up to believe that God expected me to behave in certain ways. There were things God wanted me to do (such as read the Bible, attend church regularly, follow a regimen of daily devotions, be respectful to those in authority). There were patterns of behavior God preferred I avoid, such as hanging around pool halls, swearing, frivolous pursuits (especially on Sunday), and getting too friendly with girls. I thought it reasonable then that anyone who claimed to be a Christian should express the tenets of his faith through the shape and tone and texture of his life, and I still think so. A religion which consists in a set of convictions or periodic worship or mystical experience but never marches out of the mind and heart's private sanctuary to give structure to our encounter with the world isn't much of a faith. I can't recall meeting a Middle-Class Christian, either as a boy growing up in an MCC culture or as a pastor of MCC churches, who doubted that our faith should produce a distinctive life style, although we didn't call it life style until rather recently.

Also, while there were minor sectarian variations and regional differences in MCC definitions of the definitive Christian life style, these definitions were more notable for their agreements than for their discrepancies. I know I grew up with a rather clear picture in my mind of what kind of person a Christian was supposed to be and suffered from spiritual cramps whenever I deviated from it. I can remember quite accurately its outline and herewith reproduce it.

1. A Christian is sober, industrious, and thrifty (John Wesley said you should save all you can).

2. A Christian is a solid supporter of church and community.

3. A Christian reads the Bible and prays regularly, preferably by a fixed schedule.

4. A Christian can permit himself reasonable comfort, but he is suspicious of opulence and conspicuous consumption.

5. A Christian is clean (John Wesley said cleanliness is next to godliness), neat in appearance, and avoids extremes in hair styles and haberdashery (the stricture on hair style does not apply rigorously to female Christians, and the female Christian has more latitude in apparel than the male Christian, but she must always be modest and never provocative in her attire).

6. A Christian may eat heartily (even gluttonously) of plain, wholesome food, but a taste for overly fancy viands (especially French cuisine) is a snobbish affectation and is often a symptom of decadent fleshly appetites.

The Case of a Middle-Class Christian

7. A Christian regards sex as about the most dangerous thing in life. Jesus didn't have any sex experience at all, but God doesn't demand that we quite live up to that standard. Copulation is permissible and even good when practiced with restraint by married couples. All other sexual activity is evil and, if indulged in, must be repented and abandoned before you are acceptable to God. God especially hates homosexuals, and they have to repent and shape up as heterosexuals (in orientation, not necessarily in practice) before God can like them. Judicious practice of birth control is to be encouraged because it is uneconomic for a couple to have too many children. Divorce is permissible in certain circumstances, but divorced persons cannot be looked on as quite equal in virtue to those who have not been divorced.

8. God approves wholesome recreation. Examples of wholesome recreation are wholesome plays and movies, picnics, any kind of sports, reading wholesome books, church suppers, well-chaperoned school dances, fishing, shooting rabbits, squirrels, and pheasants with shotguns. Examples of unwholesome recreation are attending stag movies and burlesque shows, reading unwholesome books, gambling, dating a girl who will let you put your hand under her dress or worse, the use of beverage alcohol (the use of drugs would have been proscribed too, but when I was growing up the only people we knew who used drugs were Dr. Fu Manchu who smoked opium and Sherlock Holmes who mainlined a little morphine now and then).

9. Christians are opposed to war on principle, but when our country gets in one it is a Christian's duty to support it and fight in it if he is able because our country is always on the side of justice and right in any war we fight. (My parents, I should say, while not doctrinaire pacifists, never quite bought this proposition, so I never quite bought it either.)

10. A Christian should engage in honest work according to his God-given talents. God looks on all worthy labor, from lowly manual toil to the activities of high-placed executives, as equal so long as an honest day's work is given in return for an honest day's pay. Christian businessmen and Christian professional men, though, deserve an extra measure of approval (so long as they tithe their income) because they strive with extra diligence to provide either economic benefits to the community or necessary services to people. The Christian ministry is not a profession but a calling, and those who respond to the call are quite naturally God's special favorites.

Reflecting on how I scored on the MCC life-style test, I decided that I deserved a grade of C.

On point one I didn't do well at all. I was sober enough if that means I took life seriously. I was industrious only in those activities (such as sports) which interested me. I never did get the hang of thrift because, I suppose, I inherited from my parents the conviction that money is essentially something to spend instead of something to save. As I grew up our family suffered from the depression-induced impecuniosity which was the lot of the middle class, but I was never denied anything I needed in favor of swelling the savings account.

Continuing down the check list: I supported church and community insofar as I wasn't an anarchist trying to blow up things; I prayed some, had an occasional go at reading the Scriptures, but never managed a fixed devotional schedule; never strove for sinful opulence because there was no chance of achieving it anyway; was strong on cleanliness (you take a shower every day after football or basketball or track practice); had a liking for snappy (but not bizarre) clothes; wasn't tempted by immoral continental cuisines because no one in my circle knew what they were; participated in the approved wholesome recre-

67

ations as well as the prohibited unwholesome recreations; chug-a-lugged alcoholic beverages now and then, largely because my elders viewed it as wicked and my peers as delightfully devilish; and entered the Christian ministry. In sum, people didn't point to me as the ideal young Middle-Class Christian, but so far as I can recall, no one predicted I would be hung.

I now know that these rubrics of approved behavior coalesced the wise, the shrewd, and the ridiculous; but as I was absorbing them into my bones, I assumed that they represented divine mandate.

Quite recently I was invited to address the Rotary Club ladies and guest night in the town where I spent my high-school years, which is the time in our life when we begin to understand what our society expects of us. Many of my high-school buddies, acquaintances, and girl friends were in the audience, and I had opportunity to chat with them before and after the meeting. They are now the leaders of this prosperous county seat community in northern Indiana. What impressed me most about coming back to my hometown after an interval of thirty-five years was not how much had changed but how little, especially the ideas held by the community. Although it has relaxed its attitudes toward the social use of alcohol and isn't so strong on devotional habits as it was in my high-school days, the community still holds to the essential MCC life-style ideal it held to thirty-five years ago.

My first reaction was one of overweening spiritual pride. These friends of my youth had stayed stuck in the same old cultural and spiritual mud for three decades and more while I, a liberated spirit, had moved around in the world, upgraded my understanding of life, and shucked off the shackles of stodgy MCC attitudes. My second reaction, after a comparison of my present convictions about Christian life style and my high-school classmates' convictions, was a chagrined admission that my present convictions are not so very much different from theirs.

For example, honest scrutiny of my life-style standards reveal that I don't really trust people who aren't well bathed and well barbered; that clothing which deviates radically from what I wear stimulates in me a suspicion of the wearer's mental processes; that grammatically correct speech patterns are the norm, and that the colorful idiom of the counterculture or the inflection and pronunciation of ethnics is to be regretted; that sex, while great fun, is a human weakness and we have to be somewhat wary of it; that people who own a couple of Cadillacs and a hundred-thousand-dollar house are sybarites; that anyone who is not engaged in an economically productive and socially respected occupation is a parasite and simply doesn't understand what God expects of him; that the institutions of business, religion, politics, and education, while often ineffective, faithless to their purposes, and even venal, are necessary to a stable society and should be criticized constructively but not uprooted; and that the Protestant ethic produces the kind of people and the kind of society God prefers, and without question creates the culture in which I feel most comfortable.

Now I reject many of these convictions with my mind. I am able to see quite clearly the absurdity of making superficialities such as costume and barbering the measure of a person. There is nothing in the New Testament to indicate that Jesus bathed daily, no matter what John Wesley said about cleanliness and godliness. To regard sex as a human weakness is to deny the biblical doctrine of creation. And hard work and frugality are not the only ends for life, or even the best ends.

I know all this in my head. But the arteries of my superego are so clogged with the cholesterol of inherited biases that I can't harmonize my rational and emotional attitudes toward Christian life style. Middle-Class Christians who reflect at all on a world which appears to be discarding the patterns they were taught to imitate find themselves, I believe, in the same boat with me.

Yet the churches keep telling us there is a distinctive Christian life style (which, it turns out, is the MCC life style). This strikes me as witless, preposterous, and even wicked.

It is witless because a genuine life style grows from the inside out. You believe something, and your belief causes you to behave a certain way. Some pietist sects depend on the horse and buggy for transportation—not because they prefer the horse and buggy, but because they regard the automobile as a worldly artifact, and their faith enjoins them against worldliness. We may think them odd, but their life style is authentic in that their outward behavior is an observable manifestation of their inward belief.

Trying to persuade people to adopt a Christian life style is reversing the procedure. It begins with the outside and assumes that if you can get people to look like Christians they will be Christians. It is analogous to the advertising which tells a grocery clerk that if he will use this after-shave or that hair dressing he will be transformed into a suave, sophisticated devil with the ladies. The after-shave and hair dressing probably won't hurt him and may even improve him a little, but they won't transform him. He's just a better-smelling grocery clerk with neater hair. Just so, you can't manufacture Christians by papering them with what you think are Christian patterns of behavior, although Middle-Class Christianity has always operated in the confidence that you can.

I have to assume that MCC life style is one legitimate expression of the Christian faith because it is the life style I follow and in which I am comfortable. To hold that it isn't legitimate is, for me, unthinkable because that would exclude me from the fold. I admit it has some Christian flaws in it. For example, how can I reconcile modern American MCC life style which emphasizes living safely within the parameters of calculating goodness and prudent behavior with Jesus' call for total commitment and radical action? The answer is that I can't. All I can do is to mumble something about times being different now than in first-century Palestine.

Maybe God will let me get by with my MCC life style, even considering some of its incongruities with the gospel. What he won't let me get by with is insisting that my Christian life style is normative for all Christians and the ideal toward which they should move. That is preposterous. It is also wicked because it is my claiming that I am the example for others, which is the worst form of spiritual pride.

I have no intention of abandoning my personal MCC life style and hope it will pass muster in the Holy City. I am too deeply sunk into its pleasant ruts. A Christian commune, of which there are plenty in operation around the country, or the hippie-like existence of the Jesus people demand a style of daily existence from their adherents which is in absolute contrast to my living habits, and I view their ways with distaste. But because Christian communes or Christian hippie life style aren't my bag doesn't mean that they are inauthentic expressions of the faith.

Middle-Class Christians, on the whole, are convinced that if everyone would adopt the MCC life style the result would be desirable.

Would it?

If everyone could be persuaded to behave like us MCCs, there would be a marked decrease in muggings, rapes, auto theft, and the various forms of street violence. Those are the crimes favored by the lower classes. This would be desirable. Whether it would reduce white-collar crime such as embezzlement, stock manipulation, bribing public officials, suborning juries, and so on, all of which is a near-monopoly of the middle and upper classes, and which is therefore looked on as socially superior to armed robbery, is doubtful.

There would be other social benefits, too. There would be a growth in respect for authority. There would be an increase in support for the presently beleaguered institutions of society. It would shore up the sagging fortunes of the family. A middle-class Christian society would pay us dividends in stability, uniformity, and smoothness of operation.

Would such changes be improvements? I think so, and I doubt that very many sensible MCCs would disagree with me, even though the stabilization of contemporary society is not a noticeable New Testament goal for Christians.

But there are catches to creating a standard life style. One of them is that when you create conformity you create drabness. Assessed objectively, we MCCs are a colorless lot. We suppress, when we can, the novel, the outrageous, the scintillations of fools and geniuses, the exciting, the challenging, the bizarre, the colorful, the tragic, and the sublime. The effort to convert everyone to a Christian life style is an exercise in leveling up and leveling down, its goal a bland and predictable people.

I do not know that blandness and predictability are sinful, but I do know that they are uninteresting. My extensive experience as a chaplain to Middle-Class Christians has convinced me that the MCC insistence on conformity to a drab life style eliminates more potential converts than any one other item in our catalogue. People who are attracted to the precepts of the faith are repelled by our narrow definitions of how the faith must be lived out in the world. This would be O.K. if MCC life style were the only authentic Christian option, as we pretend that it is. But it isn't, and there's the catch.

Another catch is that when you try to produce an homogenous culture, just as when you try to breed an homogenous race, you can end up with a species that looks and acts like you want it to but is more vulnerable to strange viruses than mixed breeds. A mongrel pup is better fitted to survive in the world than a purebred champion of the Westchester dog show. A mongrel culture will stay alive a lot longer than a culture bred to an ideal, Christian or otherwise, because it has the capacity to admit and assimilate the strengths of other strains. One reason for the durability of the Roman Catholic church, whether you think that desirable or not, is its traditional tolerance of cultural variety. It believes the church is monolithic, but it recognizes that Christian life style isn't.

When it comes to the Christian life-style game, it seems that Middle-Class Christians don't know how to play it, but they pretend that they make up the rules. But it is too big a game to remain undefined.

I don't know that it is the case, but maybe we MCCs are reluctant to wrestle with the troublesome specific questions as to acceptable or authentic life style. Maybe we feel threatened by beards and soiled raiment and unconventional living arrangements because they symbolize the really serious questions for which we have failed to provide Christian answers.

There are a number of life-style questions which beg for honest confrontation by us MCCs, but we aren't going to get a hit in this game until we dig in and swing at the questions about sex that are being pitched at us. Here are some of them.

Are sexual relationships sanctified by legal and/or

ecclesiastical blessing, or are they sanctified by love, tenderness, and mutual concern? Don't try to weasel out by saying both. Which one has priority?

Let's ask ourselves some specific questions which will reveal our true attitude toward the above question.

1. Does God prefer a loveless, brutal sexual relationship within marriage to a loving relationship outside marriage?

2. Should children be taught that any sexual relationship outside of marriage is sinful?

3. Can, and should, young people be convinced that a marriage license and a preacher converts what it is very bad for them to do into what is very good for them to do?

4. Is masturbation unchristian?

5. Is the Christian solution to the problem of the engaged couple who must postpone marriage for economic or educational reasons also to postpone sexual relations?

6. Should adolescents and preadolescents be taught frankly and honestly about sex? Should they be exposed to teaching films such as those prepared by the Unitarian-Universalist church which depict actual sex acts?

7. Can homosexuals be Christians?

8. Can the church or a church legitimately exclude homosexuals from the fellowship simply because they are homosexuals?

9. Are there any modes of sexual relations between consenting adults that are unchristian per se? If your answer to this question is yes, then list the modes of sexual expression which are not permitted a Christian.

10. If a mother knows her unmarried daughter is engaging in intercourse with a boy or boys, would it be more Christian to punish the daughter and attempt to limit her contacts with boys than to provide her with birth control information and equipment? (Studies show that

modern teenagers are woefully ignorant of and not much concerned about contraception.)

You have to answer these questions yes or no because people today, especially young people, are insisting on yes or no answers from the church. When I was a pastor to MCCs, I had to face these questions, and what I did was to hedge and hum and haw. I knew that the prescribed and approved MCC answers were yes to questions 1 through 5; the answers to 6 and 7 were no; and the answers to 8, 9, and 10 were yes. I equivocated because I wasn't sure I knew all the answers and because I knew that no deviation from the MCC answers would be tolerated by the congregation.

The MCC church, in my judgment, can't get away with such backing and filling on the subject of sex—not today it can't. I came out of seminary thoroughly confident that the holy negatives my inherited MCC perspective had provided me on the subject of sex were all the answers I would ever need as a pastoral counselor. To my amazement the problems of love, marriage, and sex brought to me for untangling were varied beyond my imagining, and my copybook counseling soon ran out of answers. I expect seminaries today do a better job preparing their students for coping with sex counseling than they did when I was in one. My seminary didn't prepare me at all.

My personal estimate, though, is that Middle-Class Christianity is not yet ready to deal with sex as we find it in the real world.

A year or so ago one of the country's most prominent seminaries employed a teaching film about homosexuality for the purpose of fitting future pastors to handle the counseling of homosexuals which, the world being what it is, would inevitably be a part of their parish responsibilities. What happened was that one of the exceedingly pious students was horrified (one is tempted to speculate as to

The Case of a Middle-Class Christian

the roots of his reaction) and reported to the press what was going on. The press, which recognizes news when it sees it, gave the story a big play. As I could have guessed, and you could too, the churches of the seminary's sectarian persuasion erupted in violent condemnation. They didn't deny the existence of homosexuality, but these Middle-Class Christians preferred to pretend that it didn't exist, or at least pretend that it was none of the church's business.

My gloomy conclusion is that Middle-Class Christianity just isn't ready yet to deal honestly and openly with the subject of faith and sex. Modern frankness has made sex mentionable, but we still are uncomfortable with it.

But where can the Christian turn for certifiable Christian guidance on the regulation of his sexual life style?

One Christian lady assured me that the Ten Commandments contained all the information on sexual conduct a Christian would ever need. What she meant was what she thought the Decalogue said about sex was adequate for Christians. She was unaware that its strictures against adultery and coveting a neighbor's wife were designed to protect a man's investment in his female chattel and had nothing to do with chastity. Leviticus orders us to kill homosexuals, and though I recently read a "letter to the editor" in which the writer enthusiastically approved this course, not many of us would sanction such an approach to the problem. Probably the Old Testament isn't a rich source of specific information in a quest for Christian sexual ethics, although Song of Songs does have its points.

And the New Testament is surprisingly shy on spelled-out sexual advice. In some places Jesus appears to be quite rigid in his attitudes toward divorce, but in other places he softens this attitude. In some places he insists on the repression of sexual urges, but in others he seems to be more permissive. Christians who try to fashion a sexual ethic from Jesus' specific sayings on the subject usually end entangled in sophistries. I yield to no man in admiration for St. Paul. However, his obvious hang-ups about sex, plus his expectation of an early apocalypse, render him an uncertain guide in this area.

Nor am I nominating myself as the fashioner of an authentic Christian sexual ethic. My hang-ups are not the same as St. Paul's, but I have them. As noted, they were handed down to me as a part of the luggage of MCC culture, and I won't ever be entirely rid of them. They are bound to contort or color any answers I would furnish. So I'm not going to set forth the new Christian sex ethic and life style for you.

I am, however, going to suggest the way to go about it.

First, we ought to begin all over again. To begin again, we start by throwing out the standard MCC holy negatives which have constituted about all we have had to say on the subject. What's good about them (and I think there is some good although you have to remember my biases) will be recovered in shaping a new ethic.

Second, I believe that despite its shortage of specific guidance on the subject, any Christian sex ethic and life style must be biblically based. I would use the Old Testament's clear statement that what God has made (including boys and girls) is good and is not to be thought of as evil. We Middle-Class Christians have never gotten this simple teaching through our heads, much less our hearts.

Then I would add the New Testament's clear emphasis on healing and wholeness and full humanity, on Jesus' concern for people as people, on his proclamation that he came to bring us an abundant life. This biblical combination would be the foundation on which I would build a new Christian sex ethic. It is a sturdy and unsentimental footing.

Actually, we'd be better off to abandon the life-style game. We'd best quit worrying about the precise manner in which a Christian behaves and address ourselves to the discovery of what it is mandatory for a Christian to believe (which will probably turn out to be less than we imagine it will be). Then we can grow our life style from the inside out.

What we'll find out is that Christians can sprout a profusion of patterns for living, varied in appearance, diverse in day-to-day behavior, wide-ranging in style, but all legitimately Christian because all are tethered to Christian convictions.

We have somehow come to believe that there is a perfect model Christian life style, but there isn't. If there were, it would have to be found in the configurations of Jesus' daily existence, but no Christian I know—middle class or otherwise—tries to reproduce in his life style the life style of Jesus. So let's quit kidding ourselves that Christian life style is closed-ended, bounded by the ethical and aesthetic perspectives of Middle-Class Christianity. It isn't closed-ended, it's open-ended, and the rich possibilities of the Christian's living out his faith in the world we have only begun to explore.

Chapter Seven

ON
BEING IN LOVE
WITH
THE NICENE CREED

ONE OF MY COLLEGE CLASSMATES, who entered the ministry of some theologically right-wing Presbyterian sect, got himself into a brouhaha over—of all things—the Nicene Creed.

If I recall the circumstances correctly, he attempted to expel a deacon of his congregation because the fellow acknowledged that Christ was "very God" but wouldn't affirm that Christ was "very God of very God." It sounds like such sublime nonsense that you probably think I made it up, but I didn't.

On campus I knew him only slightly because I sought the companionship of freer spirits and also because he wasn't a very likable guy. The impression of him that I am able to resurrect after more than thirty years of not thinking about him at all is of a tall, lean, humorless, loveless young man who had the beady eyes of those who get their information direct from another world.

But my impression is wrong on one count. He wasn't loveless. He didn't appear even to like any people, but he had fallen in love with the Nicene Creed.

I grew up believing that creeds, while not necessarily

things I should fall in love with, were awfully important to the Christian. My MCC heritage was shot through with sacred formulas, shibboleths of salvation, the orotund clichés of faith. Now no healthy teen-ager takes any of these very seriously. He hears them repeated, extolled, and urged upon him if he is brought up in a standard-brand MCC church, but he doesn't think about them much, one way or the other. The current Jesus movement, with all those adolescents and postadolescents in their scruffy jeans and fringed shirts toting Bibles and yelling about the blood of Jesus, scares me a little because it is a sick kid who is attracted by creeds and salvation prescriptions, and that's no way to get well.

I wasn't taught to love the Nicene Creed, but I was taught that one must subscribe to the Apostles' Creed if he expects to be included in the circle. If my intellectual history was like I now think it was, my shifting relationship to the Apostles' Creed began by learning to mumble it from memory without thinking about it; progressed to mild speculation as to the mechanics of the virgin birth; a passing puzzlement over what the communion of saints was all about; a rejection of the whole thing as irrelevant; to my present attitude which is a combination of admiration and an inability to affirm some items in it if they mean precisely what they say.

As creeds go, the Apostles' Creed is a dandy. I was a grown man before I found out that the apostles had nothing to do with it, that it was a baptismal formula dating from the third or fourth century, I forget which, but you could look it up, and that it was an attempt to state with economy and concision what orthodox Christianity insists the faithful must believe. It is mercifully brief, has a poetic rhythm, and is easy to memorize. Ever since the Apostles' Creed was promulgated, creeds have been going downhill. I have even tried my hand at writing creeds;

and while some of mine I gauge to be first rate, I haven't even approached the felicity of phrase and the overall literary quality of the nameless author or authors of the Apostles' Creed.

In my Methodist ghetto the Apostles' Creed along with the Lord's Prayer were the pivots on which the nonsermonic segments of the Sunday morning service swung. The sermon was central, of course. I have heard countless Methodist clergymen refer to hymn, creed, and prayer as "the preliminaries," which was not so much a derogation of creeds and prayers as an understandable if often unwarranted high estimate of their own preaching. Making the sermon the shimmering jewel set in a filigree of worship whose purpose is to heighten the jewel's sparkle is only good Protestant tradition. We still knew that creed and prayer were important. For Methodists the Apostles' Creed was a constant. We were also supposed to honor John Wesley's Twenty-Five Articles of Religion although even the preachers were vague about what they said, and most Methodist ladies were pleasantly oblivious to the article which condemns the wearing of jewelery and costly apparel. We also subscribed to the belief that Christ was our personal savior, that the Ten Commandments were the individual's guide to moral conduct, that the Bible was God's authentic word, and to other shards of dogma which were tossed at us from time to time, mostly from the pulpit, sometimes in Sunday school.

Early on I discovered that the important thing about creeds and dogmas is that you believe them. It isn't at all necessary to understand them. Their affirmation constitutes the *rites de passage* into the faith and a continuing loyalty check on those who are already in. My father, had he been pressed, would have defended vigorously the accuracy of the Apostles' Creed, the necessity of guilt-induced repentance from sin as a prelude to salvation, and even the rightness of Wesley's twenty-five articles. But dogmas weren't important to him at all, and so far as I could tell had no direct influence on the way he lived. He may have professed to find the heart of the faith in its doctrines popular with middle-class evangelical Protestant Christianity, but the focus of his life and ministry was on kindness, tolerance, and helpfulness. If he were God, I'm certain he would never have excluded anyone from heaven for failing to assent to some shred of doctrine, or for that matter, the entire fabric of formal belief. In fact, he probably wouldn't have kept anyone out, except maybe the bureaucracy of the Methodist church, whose judgment and sanity he constantly questioned even though, from time to time, he was a part of it himself.

So I grew up reflecting my father's observable if not articulated conviction that creeds and doctrines are good things to have around but they shouldn't be allowed to interfere with real life. I expect this is the average MCC's estimate of creeds and doctrines, and on the whole I think it a sound attitude. My father was much better than his theology. He never got up in the morning saying, "Well, another day in which to express the Nicene formulation of the faith," or "How can I best conduct myself this day as to demonstrate that Christ was very God of very God?" More likely he threw back the covers thanking God for the new day and the excellent breakfast that was just in the offing and for all the interesting things he had to occupy him, which is what any sensible Christian would do.

As previously mentioned, a recent survey of the present attitudes of U.S. and Canadian Middle-Class Protestant Christians shows that by overwhelming numbers we do not want the historic statements of faith such as the Apostles' Creed updated, reinterpreted, or tampered with in any way. Some people are saying that this means most of us really do believe our creeds after all and that we cherish the faith as contained in these beloved formulations.

It doesn't mean that at all. It means that we are reassured by the familiar even when we don't understand it, that we are suspicious of change in the resonances of devotion, that the sound of the liturgy supports the structure, and that the whole works will tumble if the vibrations are altered.

It is analogous to the storm of protests from Roman Catholics who didn't understand a word of Latin when the mass was changed to the vernacular. It has nothing to do with belief or a passion for doctrinal precision. It has to do with spiritual complacency.

Not that the poor screwed-up chap who fell in love with the Nicene Creed is the only such Christian alive. I met plenty of them in the itinerant evangelists who pestered us with protracted meetings in their circus tents pitched on the village green and to which the churches of the community gave tepid support. I recall a number of fiery-eyed laymen who, across the years, bored me numb with their explications of triune baptism or the experience of a third work of grace or other antic dogmas, which I have mercifully forgotten, as essential to salvation. I met one recently on a television talk show, a nice-looking young pastor who spent his allotted time proving that no one is acceptable to Jehovah who refuses to confess that Christ is "the one perfect blood sacrifice for sin," and who spoke of the love of God with a snarl.

But these are the eccentrics of the faith, nonresilient spirits whose tenuous hold on reality requires undeviating loyalty to rigid doctrine. They aren't amusing, but—praise God—they aren't typical of Middle-Class Christianity.

Happily, not very many MCCs are willing to die for a dogma. You would have to be some kind of nut to lay

The Case of a Middle-Class Christian

your head on the block for the doctrine of the Holy Trinity or go to the scaffold rather than recant the Westminster Confession.

The question arises, then, if creeds are of any use at all. Yes, some. Creeds are, essentially, statements of what some people believed at the point in history when they were written.

For example, there were other creedal expressions of the faith competing with the one that finally was adopted at Nicaea. However, using parliamentary tactics and political muscle which would have appalled one of Mayor Daley's ward heelers, the proponents of what we now revere as the Nicene Creed pushed it through to adoption. It may have been the Holy Spirit at work at Nicaea, as people in love with the Nicene Creed contend, but one hesitates to ascribe such chicanery to a member of the Trinity. Most of us would prefer to say that the Nicene Creed represents the majority view at the Council of Nicaea in the year A.D. 325 (and even that is stretching the facts a bit). It is, then, not eternal truth traced by the finger of Yahweh, but an important signpost along the road of the faith.

The Christian faith is a developing religion. The Bible is evidence of this. It's a long way from Psalm 137 to the Sermon on the Mount, but the psalm is a station on the road. Even assuming that every creed and dogma possessed by the Christian faith is inerrant (which you can't assume), they aren't exhaustive. New light will be coming in, or what are theologians and preachers for?

I think most Middle-Class Christians believe this to be true, and it is a sign of health. We may thrill to the tales of Christians who died rather than recant a dogma. We have been taught to revere these martyrs, but hardly any of us want to be one. Let's quit pretending, then, that creeds and dogmas and doctrines are terribly precious to us. Let's get out into the open our true attitude, which is that, at most, our assent to them is a mild assent. Most of us have an emotional attachment to these familiar and historical formulations of the faith and the pleasant sense of certainty and permanence their repetition gives us.

But we don't live by the items of belief contained in a baptismal formula written more than sixteen hundred years ago. We aren't in love with the Nicene Creed. Even if we should be (a dubious proposition), we aren't.

The only creed, doctrine, or dogma that means any-thing at all is the one you believe wholeheartedly right now, the one on which you are willing to hinge your life, the one that you believe holds up when you check it against the world of your experience.

That's the creed which you can write today, sign it, and add an honest amen.

Chapter Eight

CHURCH, ANYONE?

I GREW UP BELIEVING that life's important reference points were home, school, and church. I never said, or even thought, "Life's important reference points are home, school, and church." They were just there. That was how things were. That was the way all Middle-Class Christians organized their lives.

Had anyone forced me to name the least important, to me, of these three fixed realities, I would have had to name the church. Home was where I ate and slept, where—in my case anyway—my life was blessed with love and concern and guidance. School was where I found identity as an athlete and class officer and member of various peer groups and, incidentally, learned a little something now and then.

Church, on the other hand, was just a part of the scene. Being a preacher's kid I resented some of the handicaps hung on my behavior by my status. It never seemed quite fair to me that because my father was pastor of the leading church in the community my personal conduct was subject to inspection and comment from which my contemporaries of lay families were exempt. My parents, though, were wise enough to be semipermissive, and I didn't grow up hating the church as so many parsonage youngsters do.

Trying to get in focus my early appraisal of the church, I get a picture of an institution that was not of any vital interest to me. I assumed, I guess, that it was the repository and dispenser of truth about God and Jesus, the definer of what constituted sin, the rules-maker for personal conduct, and something all respectable people belonged to.

My father was a superb speaker, and his sermons were anecdotal, humorous, and mightily entertaining, so I didn't mind Sunday services. Sunday school consisted of a teacher almost totally ignorant of what he was trying to teach us hurling chunks of misinformation at us. Sunday school could do awesome damage to a kid's attitude toward Christianity if kids paid any attention to what is being taught, but fortunately they seldom do. The Sunday evening youth meeting, which in those days the Methodists called the Epworth League, was mainly a place to make connections with a girl.

I grew up, then, with an image of the church as a sedate community institution whose purpose was to articulate and sanction current cultural values, which is a fair description of what the church has been ever since it got out of the catacombs and cabbaged onto most-favored status under the Emperor Constantine back in the fourth century. This is how MCCs think of the church today and what they expect their particular church to be. This accounts for the plethora of impressive and expensive-to-maintain church buildings in almost every American town and city, because how can you expect to sanction current culture and make it stick unless you do it from a place which, if not as permanent as Sinai, at least looks solid enough to command respect? This explains the MCC horror of the counterculture or any radical deviation of thought and behavior from MCC standards, because when you ignore Middle-Class Christian standards you are thwarting God.

This explains, too, why the standard-brand MCC churches—from mainline conservative to fashionable liberal denominations—are shrinking at an accelerating rate, or partly explains it anyway. Americans have apparently rejected the notion that the Christian faith is congruent with Middle-Class Christian culture. The conviction that our values are God's values, which was once our strength, is now our undoing.

If I were running a church today and didn't care about anything but making it a booming institutional success, I know what I would do. I would espouse and preach a narrow, even outlandish theology based on what I would claim to be the only accurate interpretation of the Bible's message. It wouldn't make the slightest bit of difference how nutty, inconsistent, or off-base my theology was so long as it was narrow and excluded from the benefits of salvation anyone who failed to subscribe, *in toto,* to it and who neglected to give passionate support in time and money (lots of money) to my organization. I would talk all the time about the imminent return of Jesus (if Jesus is coming again any minute, there is no point, as St. Paul saw, in getting worked up over what is happening in the world because it will soon be gone anyway). I would build a plain pipe-rack type of building but would hire the best musicians and most charismatic youth director I could find because zingy music and a popular youth director who is saving our young people are great income producers. I wouldn't say much about the love of God— in fact, I wouldn't say anything about it—but would bear down all the time on the wrath of God. I would make the winning of others to my church and its message the first responsibility of my followers, even insisting that their salvation is dependent on their evangelistic labors. I would constantly denounce modernism and never forget that the key word in my vocabulary is *old*—the old book, the old faith, the old religion. Any point I wanted to make I would call God's law, because who's to argue with me? And whatever name I gave my church or movement, I would modify with some variation of the phrase *Bible believing*. I couldn't miss.

It isn't that I'm so smart to have figured this out. All I have to do is observe the churches which are prospering today. Most of them look like what I have described. Some are more sophisticated and subtle in their methods than others. Some of these successful churches are led by people who sincerely believe what they are preaching. Others are managed by out-and-out charlatans who are smart enough to perceive that the wave of the future, so far as institutional religion is concerned, is the backwash of the past.

The current prosperity of conservative religion, as well as the rapid erosion of standard-brand MCC sects, has been amply documented. The statistical graphs of all mainline denominations—Roman Catholic, Presbyterian, Methodist, Episcopalian, Lutheran—look like the Dow-Jones chart in a bear market. Even the Southern Baptists, who are conservative and evangelical and in tune with the religious mood of the day, while still growing, are losing some steam as indicated by a declining rate of growth. But business was never better in the independent tabernacle, the local Bible church, the supermarket-style structure with a neon cross and the proclamation that "we preach the blood, the book, and the blessed hope." Pastors of some of these independent tabernacle-type operations own fleets of Cadillacs and jet planes and belong to the better downtown clubs.

What does all this mean for the Middle-Class Chris-

89

tian? Should he abandon his present affiliation and join the conservative sect of his choice? Should he try to push his own standard-brand church in a conservative direction, hoping to increase business? Should he just forget the whole thing?

Some people will go for the first option and switch affiliations, but I doubt if many MCCs will bring themselves to do this. The typical Middle-Class Christian may be in ideological agreement with the conservative sects, but he is not emotionally fitted to find membership in one of them congenial. If for no other reason, he will reject this course of action because of the negative status conferred by identifying with a fringe group. He expects his church to be socially respectable, and this admittedly somewhat ignoble consideration is likely to keep him out of a conservative sect.

He is much more apt to push his particular church to imitate the message of the conservative group down the street which is bulging with people and zeal, but at the same time retain the trappings of MCC churchiness (impressive building, fine choirs, dignified worship) because he finds the sect's rather jazzy approach to public worship distasteful. My own feeling is that going conservative in a mainline church might work, but not very long and not very well. It is just like the mod services with guitars and folk songs and the like which many MCC churches embrace for awhile—it creates some interest for the moment, but enough is enough. The MCC temperament doesn't respond—or not for long—to novel and extreme theologies or cultural expressions of the faith. He may be by nature a conservative, but not that kind of a conservative.

Then should he just forget the whole thing, drop out, quit worrying about his church, let it peter out?

My own assessment, based on unscientific observation

and extensive personal acquaintance with vast numbers of Middle-Class Christians, is that the declining health of MCC denominations is partly attributable to what we might call semidropoutitis. The Middle-Class Christian doesn't forget about the whole thing, but he sort of forgets about it.

Take the case of Joe and Flo, friends of mine. Joe and Flo (not their names, of course—nobody named Joe would ever marry somebody named Flo, or vice versa) are middle aged, moderately prosperous, politically conservative, conventional in life style, respected in the community. They have belonged to the same church for well over a quarter of a century. They have served on boards, committees, financial canvasses. They have been loyal supporters of every pastor. They have always attended Sunday services with regularity. The church has been important in their lives, and they have never questioned its worth. A community without their kind of church is to them unthinkable.

But Joe and Flo aren't as hung up on church as they once were. They don't accept official positions any more. They won't work in a financial canvass any more, no matter how much the pastor badgers them. They still go to church, except when other affairs keep them away, which is about half the time nowadays. They aren't sore at the pastor, or upset with what goes on at the church, or anything like that. If you asked them how they feel about their church, they would affirm their loyalty. But they are semidropouts.

There isn't much point in going into the reasons why Joe and Flo aren't as interested in the church as they once were. Semidropoutitis can be caused by fatigue with churchiness, boredom, competing interests, any number of things. The significant fact is that MCCs just aren't as keen on church as they once were.

The Case of a Middle-Class Christian

Is this bad news? It is bad news to parish pastors and bishops and denominational executives and everyone whose professional life and income depends on the organized church. It is bad news to laymen who have to find the money to maintain expensive church buildings and underwrite program and personnel costs. It is bad news to young people considering the pastoral ministry as a career but, like prospective teachers and aeronautical engineers, see the job market drying up.

Or is it good news? Some people think it is. Some theologians say that, now the religious boom is over, we can inter the illusion that popular piety is a sign of religious health. They claim that the shakedown will eliminate the sacred fluff which passed for faith and leave a hard core of committed Christians which will revitalize the church.

I do not know whether it will turn out this way or not. I am too much of a Middle-Class Christian, too much of my life has been invested in the church to hear of its decline as glad tidings. But I do not regard the news as a death notice. It tells of a setback, but not necessarily of a disaster.

If the prognosticators are on the mark—and I think they are—then the years immediately ahead will see the continued attrition of MCC institutional Christianity. Added to the zero or minus growth rates already achieved by many MCC denominations will be the burden of taxes—or so the predictors say. State and local governments, ever hungry for new sources of tax revenue, will begin to levy taxes on church property. If this happens, and indications are that it will, then there will be a sharp upswing in the cost of doing business for churches. At the very least taxation will force retrenchment, church mergers, and the elimination of many big, costly plants.

Denominations, faced with falling revenues, are already making drastic cuts in their bureaucracies, and the end is not yet. Almost all mainline denominations are reducing the number of their theological seminaries. Clergy morale, already low, keeps sinking. The Roman Catholic church, thought to be a spiritual vessel impervious to the ravages of time and undamageable by external forces, appears to be breaking up like the *Titanic*.

So how should the conscientious Middle-Class Christian concerned about the fate of his church respond to the situation? I have some suggestions.

1. Because the church is in a decline is no reason to abandon it.

2. Trying to save the church in its present style, form, organization, and so on is likely to be a futile effort.

Most campaigns, crusades, renewal movements, and the like which purport to be aimed at revitalizing the faith are really designed to rejuvenate the institution *as it now is*. I was recently invited to address a group of lay leaders of various churches and accepted on the condition that I wouldn't have to give them a pep talk or reassure them that everything was just dandy with the church. "Oh, we are open to change," they said. "We will welcome a message about how the church can best adapt itself to the needs of a modern world." I'm sure they thought they meant it. But it turned out that what they were open to was a little cosmetic improvement, a new hairdo and even a face-lift for the church. They were totally resistant to any fundamental reorientation of the institution which would in any way alter the organization or the methods by which it now operates. And these were laymen.

The cosmetic approach to renewal reminds me of the Packard automobile company as it was about to expire. It tried to resuscitate itself by merging with the Studebaker company. It took the current Studebaker car, changed the grill and chrome strips, and called it a new model Packard.

The Case of a Middle-Class Christian

But underneath the slightly altered exterior it was just the old Studebaker (which hadn't been selling well either). No one was fooled. You know what happened to the Packard.

3. Don't look to projects such as the Consultation on Church Union which seek the merger of several middle-class denominations for the salvation of the church.

For most of my life I have been an enthusiast for church union. I recall that as a boy not much interested in church affairs I was puzzled by the abundance of competing sects. I was told that each denomination was founded to give witness to some facet of Christian doctrine and each continued to exist so as to keep its particular witness alive. It was apparent to my juvenile mind that this was a bit of pious fiction. My Presbyterian and Baptist friends were Presbyterians and Baptists not because they were persuaded of the merits of Calvinistic theology or passionately supported baptism by immersion. They were Presbyterians and Baptists because their parents, who didn't know anything about Calvin or care particularly about immersion either, were Presbyterians and Baptists.

As a young clergyman I supported every church union movement that came along. When Bishop Pike and Dr. Eugene Carson Blake proposed the Consultation on Church Union, they rang my bell. However, none of these merger and union projects have amounted to anything, and it is doubtful if they ever will. Church union from the top bogs down into a battle between denominational hierarchies and bureaucracies struggling to hang on to their power and prerogatives.

4. Standard-brand churches (and also off-brand churches, if possible) should seek to merge their efforts, not their organizations, at the community level.

This, of course, is what is happening now. While the Consultation on Church Union has spent more than a

decade talking about how to replace several church organizations with one whopping big church organization,
sensible Christian laymen have been learning how to work
together in their communities. They have, in effect, moved
right on past the projects for organic church union.

The Middle-Class Christian layman has a shaky grasp
of theology, is all but unacquainted with the Bible, and
is unaware of what dogmas his denomination stands for.
Preachers, myself included, often deplore the MCC layman's religious illiteracy and class it as a weakness of organized religion, which of course it is. Ironically, it is
this weakness which lends strength to the cooperative
movement. The MCC layman may not understand the in-
tricacies of predestination or the reasons why triune baptism
is essential to salvation, but he does understand the idiocy
of fifteen churches in the community all trying to dupli-
cate the others' programs. And he will respond to an
appeal to join forces in order to get a job done properly.
His lack of interest in biblical, theological, and organizational differences which are supposed to separate denominations is a great barrier-breaker.

The MCC layman possesses another characteristic
which predisposes him toward church cooperation at the
community level—his disinclination to spend money un-
necessarily. When he learns that he can get more by
spending less through pooling resources to carry on programs of Christian education, pastoral care, cooperative use
of church buildings, and so on, he is three-fourths sold
on interdenominational cooperation.

5. Insist that your church pour more of its energies into
the ministry of health and healing than it is now doing.

Yours may be that exceptional local church which is
already doing this, but the average MCC congregation
spends its substance doing a lot of things which don't need
doing, to the neglect of a genuine New Testament min-

istry in the community. I would use Jesus' ministry as the pattern, remembering that he dealt with human need where he was confronted by it and provided whatever kind of healing was called for. Most MCC churches do some genuine healings, but not nearly enough. Our activity is usually heavily weighed toward building up the organization's strength and community prestige.

You must remember that if you are going to follow Jesus' pattern you can't qualify your healing ministry and you can't calculate it so as to reflect credit on your congregation.

Read the Gospels again, and see how often the recipients of Jesus' ministry were people who had no claim on him, and in many instances were crooks, cheats, and unsavory sinners of various kinds.

The church has always been at its best when it has tackled the human problems which are being ignored by everyone else. It did precisely this when it pioneered in education. The church also was the first to do something about providing for the care of the aged through its retirement homes. Even in a state such as ours that is paved with welfare programs there are many people who slip through the gratings.

It is not my business to detail a model ministry of healing for your church. That depends on what's needed where you are and your church's willingness to do something about it. One example of the ministry of healing I know of is carried on by Marble Collegiate Church in New York City, the church of which Dr. Norman Vincent Peale is pastor. Located in an area where people have every conceivable personal crisis around the clock, the church maintains a well-staffed counseling service with a telephone switchboard manned twenty-four hours per day.

Now I admire a ministry like this. It appeals to me as a truly Christian response to the human need of a particular community. I expect, too, that if you are in a community of any size your church could well consider a program something like it. Every community I ever served needed a good, well-run, comprehensive counseling service. You may be thinking that your church couldn't afford to do this, and you are probably right. But a dozen churches in your town, or even fewer, could handle it as a cooperative project.

I am aware that the trend of the moment is for churches to withdraw from the world, to stress devotionalism and personal salvation, to save you out of the world. What I am advising bucks the trend, and if you follow my advice, it may not help build up your church or bring more people in or add to the budget. So let's revert to a little theology, even if you don't care much for theology. Answer this question: Is God at work in the world to save the world or has he given up on the world as a bad job and is interested only in saving people out of the world?

If you answer yes, God loves the world and is at work in the world—as I believe you must answer if you are at all familiar with the Bible—then to retreat into devotionalism and personal salvation is a cop out. There is nothing wrong with devotionalism for those who like it (except, maybe, it encourages some people to spiritual pride—but then, nearly everything encourages some people to spiritual pride). And personal salvation is a legitimate part of a church's emphasis. But they aren't enough by themselves for a New Testament ministry in the world. Remember that Jesus did not put the woman taken in adultery through a salvation formula nor insist that Zacchaeus attend prayer meeting.

I do not know that a bold, imaginative humanistic ministry will save the Middle-Class Christian religious institution. It may not. But it might save the MCC church's soul.

The Case of a Middle-Class Christian

6. Be confident the church isn't going to expire even though some of the present forms of the church die out.

If Middle-Class Christians could rid themselves of the idea that the demise of MCC styles of church organization is the death of the church, there would be no need for all the hand-wringing over the parlous condition of Old First Church at the corner of Main and Market. Anyone who knows a little church history knows that the community of the faithful has managed to exist in all sorts of organizational arrangements. The local parish church is a latecomer to Christian history, and denominational churches competing with one another are modern inventions. So there is no reason at all to think the Christian community, which is what the church is, won't survive the extinction of the standard MCC church.

Not that anyone expects the standard MCC church to go down the drain anytime soon. It appears to be in the process of petering out, but the process will last awhile. For many years I believed that the process could be reversed. I admit that I no longer believe this to be possible. I keep in rather close touch with what is going on in various ecclesiastical headquarters and, as yet, see no cloud of hope that among the leadership of the church there is the vitality, imagination, or perception to bring about a significant reversal. Most of the thinking which goes on in these vaticans is at about the level of the proposal I heard one church bureaucrat make to an assembly of church leaders. The way to reverse the decline, he said, is to "call a moratorium on criticism of the church."

If you really want to know what is going to happen, the place to look for the signs is among the generation which will soon be the establishment. On one university campus I know quite well the churches were overwhelmed with students as recently as five or six years ago. One of the churches most popular with students couldn't handle the crowds in three Sunday morning services. Today this church can't fill the nave half-full in one service. And this university is located not in some eastern metropolis but in a smallish community in the heart of the midwestern Bible belt, a traditional stronghold of Middle-Class Christianity.

Where have the kids gone? Some of them are to be found in the campus all-student Roman Catholic chapel. They go there because the services are very mod and because it is considered chic for Protestants to attend the R.C. church. But most of them don't go anywhere. They just don't see any reason whatever to go to church. We might hope that, once they establish families and settle in suburbia, they will reknot their broken ties with organized religion and become good churchmen. After all, a lot of us did something like that. But in the case of the present generation of college kids I think it unlikely that great numbers of them will ever come back to the church.

However, I know many young people, who, though disenchanted with MCC churchiness, are actively seeking new forms of Christian community which will be more real and more vital to them than the standard community churches.

So you should be sanguine about the future of the church. If you are satisfied with your present MCC church, then stick with it, even if it is losing steam. Be glad, though, for the new, the novel, the experimental Christian forms of organization which are springing up. They assure us that, though the style of Christian community we think of as normative for the church is taking its lumps, the faith is alive and well and quite capable of carrying on.

Chapter Nine

BAD NEWS
AND
GOOD NEWS

THE BAD NEWS about today's Middle-Class Christian is that he isn't going to change very rapidly. This is also the good news.

It is bad news because Christianity—New Testament Christianity anyway—appears to call for radical commitment of self, willingness to suffer for Christ's sake, a marked and often extravagant change in personal values and one's whole approach to life. I can't think of any MCC of my acquaintance, myself included, who comes anywhere near fitting this picture. We shy away from radical religion just as we shy away from radical politics or radical economics.

As a boy I heard numberless sermons telling me I should give myself totally to Christ. Did giving myself totally to Christ mean I should leave home and family and possessions for Christ's sake, as the Gospels suggest? No, unless I felt called to the mission field. In that case I wouldn't make any money, of course, but the pain of separation would be assuaged by plenty of native servants who would cook and clean for me and do all the grubby work that had to be done because in Africa and India servants come

100

dirt cheap. And I'd get a year's furlough home every quadrennium.

What the preachers of my nonage and youth meant by total commitment to Christ, it turned out, was that people submit to a conversion experience and adopt an intense loyalty to MCC values, including—especially including—faithfulness to the church and tithing one's income. Converts were supposed to go right on being bankers and insurance salesmen and funeral directors and grocers and members of Kiwanis and secretaries of the Parent-Teacher Association. Good churchmanship and solid citizenship, so far as I could tell, were the fruits of conversion, the flowering of total commitment to Christ.

And who's to say that they aren't? If every Middle-Class Christian took the radical demands of the New Testament literally, who'd be left to look after the store?

I confess, though, that I've always been haunted by the comparison of my comfortable, sedate existence and the radical recommendations for discipleship in the New Testament. I admire extravagantly such Christians as Albert Schweitzer and Dietrich Bonhoeffer, who gave up everything for Christ's sake, but I'm not about to imitate them. I don't have it in me. Judged by New Testament standards my commitment is flawed. I am more middle-class than I am Christian, and you are too. I suspect that our awareness of our feeble commitment, even if we don't admit it to ourselves, is the stimulus for whatever generosity we show in contributing to the church. We are willing to support others who presumably are committed enough to go out and do the Lord's work. It is a little like the once-legal practice of hiring someone to do your military service for you.

What are we MCCs to do with such texts as "Do not lay up for yourselves treasures on earth . . ."; "He who loves father or mother more than me is not worthy of me"; "Do not resist one who is evil"; "How hard it is to enter the kingdom of God"? This is radical stuff. We'd be healthier, I think, to admit that we aren't up to it. Everything in our natures, our habits, our values votes against the extreme, even extreme commitment to Christ. No amount of tricky exegesis is going to put us into conformity with New Testament standards of Christian discipleship. It has been a long time since I have paid any attention whatever to a bishop's exhortation to be a true disciple of Jesus, or the sermon of a preacher knocking down fifteen thousand per year plus house plus expense account calling us to a genuine commitment to Christ, and it will be a long time before I do. I may be a fuzzy and imperfect replica of the real thing, but I'm not going to pretend that my pleasant middle-class existence (which I intend to continue) is what Jesus had in mind when he talked about the conditions of discipleship.

As a matter of fact, I don't like extremists of any kind very well, and probably you don't either. The radical Christian liberals of my acquaintance tend to be intellectual snobs, simplistic in their solutions to problems, unrealistic in their appraisal of human nature, and quite uncharitable of their Christian brethren who do not see things as they see them. Extremely conservative Christians strike me as compassionless people whose faith is not in Christ but in narrow and dehumanized theologies, who would gladly see you in hell if you refuse to conform to their formulas.

I believe most MCCs feel as I do about radical religion, and while this distaste for the extreme may keep us from answering the New Testament call to radical discipleship, it will also prevent Middle-Class Christianity from being swamped by extremes of the theological right or left. This is the good side of our MCC middle-of-the-roadism.

My own rather lengthy experience as pastor to Middle-

Class Christians suggests that they are open to new insights if the new insights are presented in a reasonable manner. They believe in education, progress, and new ideas. What they don't believe in is radical change of any kind. If the MCC religious establishment has any future at all, it will be because it is unlikely to fall for any attempts to switch it to the radical right or the radical left. Of course, this penchant for stability can also end up in decay (and there is evidence that this is happening) unless the leadership of the establishment guides it wisely and rapidly enough into the new duties demanded by new occasions. Whether this will happen or not is yet to be determined.

Maybe we're selling the faith short when we admit we aren't going to measure up to the New Testament standards of Christian discipleship. I wouldn't argue with anyone who gives us a D in discipleship and calls us a sorry lot for Christians. I only claim it is better to confess our shortcomings and refuse to kid ourselves that we are, or are going to be, obedient to Jesus' criteria for his followers than it is to pretend that we measure up.

Maybe encouraging MCCs to a patient and continued growth in the grace and knowledge of God is the best we can hope for. It falls short of the highest forms of discipleship if we are to believe the New Testament, but it isn't the worst thing we could do.

Chapter Ten

ON
TRYING
TO
FEEL RELIGIOUS

THE PREACHING ON WHICH I was brought up told me that the measure of my state of grace was my feelings. A saved Christian (as distinguished from a nominal Christian) had, I gathered, a sense of spiritual exuberance occasioned by release from sin and the knowledge that he was headed for heaven. His feeling of being saved was maintainable by the right devotional regimen plus, of course, abstaining from the sinful habits he was supposed to forsake as a precondition of salvation.

Today a more urbane version of feeling religious preaches that faith will make you feel self-confident, positive, aggressive in striving toward personal goals, all of which will issue in success which is the greatest feeling of all. One way or another, we Middle-Class Christians have been conditioned to associate true religion with good feelings.

I think this is a lot of bunk.

One reason I think it is a lot of bunk is that, were it true, I couldn't lay claim to salvation because I have never been suffused with ecstasies of redemption. My reluctance to be excluded from the circle of the saved is, of course, selfish and certainly not a telling argument against those who claim there is no salvation unaccompanied by rapture. But if my experience is typical of nearly all Middle-Class Christians—and I think it is—then we'd have to say that surely few are chosen and that a lot of us have a problem.

Probably it is a great thing to exist in the euphoric certainty of being one of God's elect—I wouldn't know. If you are one of these, congratulations! Since I haven't experienced it, it would be ungracious of me to knock it.

Also, I admit that I've worried no little bit about this spiritual deficiency of mine although I don't worry much about it any more. But I do want to be the beneficiary of God's forgiving and redeeming grace, and I expect you do too, so we'd better come to terms with the inadequacies of our religious feelings.

Maybe we should try harder to feel religious.

If we could manage to feel more sinful than we do, perhaps we could inject more fear and trembling into our spirits, which would in turn produce a greater need for repentance than we normally feel, which would in turn insure a more marvelous and miraculous feeling of relief when we repent. This is about what the old-fashioned evangelist attempted to do for us or to us.

But it washes out as psychological manipulation whether it is done by others or self-induced. One doubts that this is what God is aiming at. Anyway, it doesn't work very well. Most of us who wear the MCC label have a history of faithfulness (in some degree) to the faith. We may be unacquainted with the heights and depths of religious feeling, but we think our hanging in there counts for something. We believe we are Christians even if we have never experienced the despair of the lost or the bliss of the rescued sinner.

I'll tell you how I handle the problem, and—if you

are like I am so far as feeling religious is concerned—how you can handle it.

Let's admit that there is what John Wesley called "the witness of the Spirit." Let's not say that religious feeling is inauthentic or undesirable. Let's regard it as a gift presented to some and withheld from others. That takes care of feeling guilty because we don't feel religious.

The important part of my solution to the problem of wanting to be in the number of the saved but not having received flashes of ecstasy or been afforded glimpses of glory is to remember that, however nice it is to feel religious, we aren't saved by our feelings. Feeling religious, however you define the term, is a sort of fringe benefit of salvation. You can get along without it.

And whenever I get to thinking I have missed it, that maybe my lack of religious feelings means I am an unregenerate, I recall that Martin Luther, a man who had a lot of trouble with this problem himself, once said, "We depend on the unseen, *unfelt*, [italics mine] and unknown goodness of God."

That's just great! It says it for me. It speaks to my condition. It comforts me like all get-out. I have this powerful inner conviction that Luther's statement corresponds to reality (which, maybe, is a form of feeling religious). As Francis Thompson said,

> His name I know
> And what His trumpet saith.

And the best thing about it is, I know it when I can't hear the trumpet.

Chapter Eleven

SHOULD YOU GO IN FOR GLOSSOLALIA?

WHEN I WAS A BOY, there was reputed to be, somewhere in our county, a group of Christians whose meetings were characterized by each member jumping around and rolling on the floor, all the while jabbering away in syllables unintelligible to the uninitiated auditor but filled with grace and meaning to those who knew these charismatic utterances to be the language of heaven. We called them Holy Rollers, and I remember my father speaking of their practices with repugnance.

After a seminary education I was aware that Holy Rollers were Christians who organized their spiritual lives around glossolalia or speaking in tongues which the New Testament mentions, although sparingly. Glossolalia is connected with the baptism of the Holy Spirit at Pentecost. Apparently there were pockets of charismatics in the early church which held that the gift of tongues was the only authentic certification of one's spirituality, or at least an imprimatur of spiritual superiority surpassing any other sign from heaven.

My first personal experience of Christians who practiced ecstatic speech came about after a good many years in the pastorate. I was located in a college town, and one of the pretheological students in the college, though preparing to enter the ministry of the Methodist church, was obsessed with glossolalia and hung around with Pentecostal groups all the time. What happened was that he persuaded the athletic director of the college to rent him the college gym for a week's meeting of all the tongues people in the area plus, he hoped, hundreds of students. The athletic director, an amiable fellow who probably hadn't been to church since his daughter's wedding, had no notion whatever of what Pentecostal Christianity was. However, he thought a dose of religion couldn't hurt the campus any and might even help tame the animal spirits of the lustier students and thus simplify life for the college administrators, especially the administrator of the athletic department.

The dean of the college and I decided to attend one of the meetings, not to pray but to observe. I recall watching the gym fill up with shabby, shapeless people, people who obviously never scored much in the game of life, people the like of which never applied for membership in my well-dressed congregation. I wondered where they all came from. I never saw them on the streets or in the stores, or if I did, I had never noticed them.

Well, it was a good show, and it had a lot more arousements in it than the semi-high-church liturgy practiced by my congregation. It began on a moderate note, with several musical groups representing various Pentecostal congregations in the area doing their numbers. There was a sort of master of ceremonies whose duties were akin to those of the warm-up man who gets the live audience at a TV show in a properly enthusiastic mood prior to the star's entrance. This fellow skillfully built the intensity of the congregation's emotions. Long before the star of the program appeared (he was a preacher I had never heard of but who, I learned later, enjoyed an enormous reputation in Pentecostal circles), I noticed that the congregation was dotted with people swaying back and forth in their seats, mumbling to themselves. What was going on onstage could have been happening on Mars. Nothing intruded on their private ecstasy. It was, of course, a very noisy service, and the star preacher, when he appeared, shouted every word of his sermon, which consisted mostly of reiterated New Testament texts on the subjects of glossolalia and divine healing and of frequent demands for assent from the assemblage (which he always got in the form of "Yes, Lord," shouted hallelujahs, and raucous amens).

As I say, it was a good show although I didn't get to witness any holy rolling, possibly because the gym was packed and there wasn't any place to roll. I went home speculating about this Christian subculture of whose existence I was only dimly aware. It was, I decided, a religion for people who would never make it into the middle class. Much as I regretted that the MCC establishment had nothing to offer these people, I was nevertheless thankful that my kind of church was impervious to whatever appeal charismatic religion had for the types attracted to Pentecostalism.

How wrong I was.

My next encounter with glossolalia was in a setting so far removed from the sweaty congregation in the college gym as to be in another world. The College of Preachers at the National Cathedral in Washington, D.C., is set up as a continuing refresher course for Protestant Episcopal clergymen who have been in service for five years or so. It occasionally admits a non-Anglican to its week-long program, and I was fortunate enough to be invited. One evening a group of us were sitting around in the very Episcopalianish library of the college when one of the bright young rectors lit up a cigarette and began a monologue in praise of the practice of glossolalia. He told of his personal involvement with the charismatic movement, of his and his congregation's experience with it, and of the spiritual blessings it brought to those who practiced it. Episcopalians, whose worship always travels on the safe rails of traditional liturgy, speaking in tongues? Incredible!

And, quite recently, we all saw on television Roman Catholic charismatics conducting a glossolalia convention at Notre Dame. Catholics speaking in tongues, at Notre Dame yet? They've got to be kidding!

It was only about fifteen years ago that I got the first hint that the practice of glossolalia was invading the staid precincts of Middle-Class Christianity (and Episcopalians are definitely Upper-Middle-Class Christians, even slopping over into the true upper class). Since then glossolalia has spread, if not rampantly at least with remarkable speed, among Lutherans, Presbyterians, Methodists, Roman Catholics, and other fortresses of Middle-Class Christianity. Friends of mine in the Methodist hierarchy tell me that they see it growing among Methodists, that hardly any area of the church is without some manifestation of it, and that before long the denomination will have to adopt some official attitude toward it.

Is glossolalia a threat or a promise? If you went in for glossolalia, now that it is practiced within the confines of respectable MCC denominations, would it recharge your spiritual batteries and make a better Christian of you? If Middle-Class Christianity officially encouraged speaking in tongues, would it bring new life and vitality to the church? If the custom of ecstatic Christian speech could do all these things, then we ought to go in for it and give it every encouragement. Here is a matter on which we can use some Christian guidance, and the best place to begin the search is the New Testament.

The experience of Pentecost as recorded by the Book of

Should You Go in for Glossolalia?

Acts definitely looks on the gift of tongues—in that particular instance—as a blessing. The descent of the Holy Spirit, inspiring as it did all present to charismatic speech, is seen as a sign from God that gentiles too were eligible recipients of divine grace.

From Pentecost on it is downhill all the way for glossolalia in the New Testament.

Most of the references to it are in Paul's first letter to the Corinthians. The Corinthians, you will remember, were a feisty bunch who caused the apostle no end of trouble. We have to assume that this was the one church most addicted to the practice of glossolalia, and that along with its corruption (through gluttony) of the Lord's Supper and the extremely permissive standards of morality among its members, it managed to turn the gift of tongues into a cause for congregational controversy.

Paul approaches the subject gingerly. He doesn't deny that speaking in tongues is numbered among the gifts of the spirit. He says, though, that it is not really a class A gift, being inferior to other gifts, especially the gift of prophecy (by which he meant intelligible instruction in the faith, not some form of Christian crystal-ball gazing). He says glossolalia generally is of benefit only to the person undergoing the ecstatic experience, and it is better to exercise gifts which are for the good of the whole church, a pretty good swipe at any brand of Christianity which reduces the faith to a purely private devotionalism. He also notes that charismatics are especially susceptible to spiritual pride, and that they shouldn't be.

I get the impression that Paul felt that glossolalia was a confounded nuisance to the church although he doesn't come right out and say so. Anyway, I hope that is what he thought about it because that is what I think about it, and I'd be in good Christian company if I am in agreement with St. Paul.

111

The Case of a Middle-Class Christian

So if you are tempted to go in for glossolalia, as a few of you may be, or if the charismatic movement gets a foothold in your standard-brand congregation, as it is doing with increasing frequency, I'd advise that you treat it as you would an epidemic of the London flu—that is, avoid being infected yourself, and cooperate in its extermination. I'm as narrow-minded on the subject of glossolalia as a hard-shell Baptist is on the necessity for total immersion.

Come to think of it, probably the best way to eradicate glossolalia would be for the MCC denominations to encourage it. That would mean organizing it, with board secretaries in charge of promoting glossolalia in the churches, and budgets, and a glossolalia magazine in four colors, and national glossolalia conventions, and all that. Institutionalizing the charismatic movement would take the starch out of it in a hurry. And that, by my lights, would be all to the good.

Chapter Twelve

ENEMY
OF
THE FAITH

FOR AS LONG AS I CAN REMEMBER, I have been hearing preachers trot out what they claimed was the number one threat to Christianity, *the* enemy of the faith, and then flog it mightily, presumably to the edification of the hearers and the strengthening of the church.

The enemy of the faith has changed with times, of course. When I was a boy *the* enemy was worldliness. Every evangelist had in his arsenal of anecdotes sad stories about, for example, the fine pure Christian girl who was an exemplar of religious virtues in her small hometown. Then she went off to the big city and shed these virtues one by one. She started to wear make-up, shortened her skirts, became a giddy devotee of ballroom dancing. She quit attending Sunday school and church. The pursuit of pleasure and a soft life finally did her in, of course. She became a "worldling," forsaking the good and true simple Christian values of her youth. The evangelists could and did switch the ending—the sin-ravaged creature who had once been the lovely Christian girl expires, regretting her worldliness. Or she is saved out of her worldliness and returns to her small town to live according to her

113

original Christian virtues. A skillful orator could get a lot of mileage out of these stories, especially the part where he described the depraved conduct of big-city types who were worldly as all get-out. I remember clearly that this was the part I liked best, and it was almost worth being bored with the rest of the sermon just for a little glimpse of the glittering wickedness in Chicago and New York and other exciting places I had never been. Worldliness sounded like great fun to me, and probably to most of the congregation, although this wasn't the effect the evangelist was trying to create.

Well, that was a long time ago, and most Middle-Class Christian congregations wouldn't know what one of those evangelists of my youth was talking about. MCC life styles in Grand Junction, Colorado, or Alliance, Ohio, do not differ markedly from the worldliness the evangelist decried. That old enemy of the faith has been laid to rest.

Maybe not quite laid to rest. A kind of modernized version of the enemy worldliness is the enemy materialism. Or, if you want to be sophisticated, you call the enemy secularism.

Materialism and secularism, in vogue as enemies of the faith when I was in seminary, still take a beating from the pulpit with some regularity. I did my share in flaying them, I blush to confess. Not that they don't have their points as enemies of the faith. The accumulation of wealth often becomes an obsession, driving any other value out of a man's life. I gather that is the lesson in the story of Jesus and the rich young ruler. And secularism, which means living by the precepts of this present age, often produces shoddy lives.

But materialism and secularism are still fake enemies of the faith. They are rooted in a dualistic concept of the world—material reality versus spiritual reality, this-worldliness versus other-worldliness. They are more the crea-

114

tions of Greek philosophy than of Christian gospel. God loves the material world he created, according to the New Testament. And while the eternal city may be our destination, we live here now.

Communism has had a pretty good run as *the* enemy of the faith, and at least one name evangelist is still exploiting it to his prosperity. But communism is another straw enemy, at least for American MCCs. I believe communism is bad stuff, but it doesn't appeal to a well-to-do society such as ours. You haven't ever met an American Communist, and you probably never will. The Communist Party, legal in the United States, is a sickly organization and is unlikely to get well.

So what is *the* enemy of the faith? What is *the* threat which can and maybe will destroy American Middle-Class Christianity?

My own judgment, based on decades of pastoring and observing Middle-Class Christians and analyzing myself as a typical MCC, is that *the* enemy of the faith is one of the seven deadly sins—specifically, the sin of sloth.

I know sloth is a strange sin with which to indict American Middle-Class Christianity. We Americans aren't lazy people, and sloth is generally thought to mean laziness. We are hyperactive. Our churches buzz and splutter with activity. We are doers, pushers, up-and-at-'em Christians.

But while the Latin word which we translate as sloth does mean "to sit idly," it can also mean "to lie fallow." You don't do any violence to this translation when you touch it up a little and make it read "spiritual laziness" or "stunted imagination" or "dullness of mind" or even "unwillingness to delve very deeply into our faith."

Somebody did some research into the quality of faith of the MCC businessman—community leader—pillar-of-his-church. The researcher discovered that MCC pastors almost unanimously liked and respected their businessmen-leaders and thought them on the whole a fine class of human beings (after all, these guys carry the load for the church), but felt that as a group they were almost oblivious to the significance of the gospel. Here are three comments from among clergymen questioned in this research.

Clergyman A: "Most of these men seem pretty well satisfied with themselves . . . [they] are abysmally ignorant of religion. They have no theology, no structure of religious thought . . ."

Clergyman B: "It is my judgment that businessmen are naïve about the intellectual basis of religion. They do not seem to care whether its theological assumptions square with experience. Their minds seem to move easily and unquestioningly in old grooves."

Clergyman C: "They always seem to shy off from anything that goes into the deeper meaning of life. You just can't get this into the program of your church."

Dullness of mind? Unwillingness to delve very deeply into our faith? The sin of sloth?

And Clergyman A, cited above, adds, "I don't think the men themselves are entirely to blame. Some of them are among the finest it has been my privilege to know. They are victims of the kind of churchmanship we have had."

What Clergyman A is saying is that a slothful church produces slothful Christians. A dull, unimaginative presentation of the gospel will not spark a vivid response from the hearers. If the pillars of Middle-Class Christianity shy off from religion that seeks to find the deeper meaning of life, as Clergyman C claims is the case, then how can Middle-Class Christianity be anything but superficial?

MC Christianity is thin religion. It is extrovert religion. It is unreflective religion.

One of the National Football League's better teams is coached by a serious, high-principled man who is among

the three or four at the top of his profession. He is a professed Christian, and so far as I know a good Christian.
The last thing the team does before leaving the locker
room is to kneel for a prayer led by the coach. One team
member is a many-times all-pro defensive lineman. A
newspaper reporter once asked this all-pro about the
team's prayer ritual.

"Do you pray to win?" the reporter asked.

"No, coach prays that we will do our best," the player
said.

"What else do you pray for?"

"Well, coach always prays that no one will get hurt in
the game today."

"Then what?"

"Then," said the player, "I go out and try to kill the
quarterback."

However sincere the prayer, this is trivial religion. It is
easy to be sincere about our faith when the faith doesn't
make much difference one way or the other. In all the long
years as an MCC pastor I hardly ever met that blatant
hypocrite whom the scoffers are so fond of citing as evidence of Christianity's essential phoniness. I knew lots of
Christians, including myself, whose performance fell below
the level of their profession, but that's normal. Our reach
should exceed our grasp. But mostly I met Christians who
sincerely held to religious convictions that didn't mean
very much—good people committing the sin of sloth.

One of the genuinely encouraging signs of hope on the
MCC horizon is that laymen are beginning to recognize
that they are guilty of sloth. The demand for programs in
the church which will enable members to understand
what the faith is all about isn't of tidal-wave proportions
by any means, but it is growing. A recent survey of the
attitudes of United Methodist laymen (and the United
Methodist Church is *the* model for American Middle-

The Case of a Middle-Class Christian

Class Christianity) showed rising expectations of their church's educational ministry. They want something more than the standard boring Sunday school lesson taught by someone who is as uninformed as they are. They suggest that biblical material and theology can best be imparted by cassettes and video tapes prepared by people who know what they are talking about instead of mumbled by some pious but ignorant teacher.

If the MCC denominations have their radars working they will detect this trend of lay thought and do something to satisfy the demand. What I am afraid of is that the denominations will blow it. Oh, they will catch the drift of lay thinking but will try to convert this thirst for deeper understanding into an institutional advantage. They will do it by providing not education but propaganda.

The difference between education and propaganda is that the propagandist knows where he wants you to come out before he begins with you and the educator doesn't. Education provides you with the best information on a subject available, then lets you decide where to go with it. The propagandist decides in advance how he thinks you should think, then arranges the information he gives you so as to lead you to his goal for you.

The churches—any of them—have never had much faith in Christian education, but much confidence in Christian propaganda. And that is the church's way of committing the sin of sloth.

If I were pope of some MCC denomination, I would pour the resources of the institution into lay instruction. I'd take advantage of technology—cassettes, video tape, things like that—to provide cheap, imaginative, and instructionally sound resources for local church programming. I'd turn some of my seminaries (most denominations have too many seminaries) into centers for continuing lay education. And I wouldn't let any denominational executive try to convert this program into a propaganda mill. In fact, I'd fire anyone who tried it. And I'm betting that, in the end, my program would be for the upbuilding of the institution—although that wouldn't be my motive for doing it.

We can't expect busy MCC laymen to submit to a seminary education or become biblical experts or theological scholars. There is no reason why they should. But they apparently are hungry to deepen their understanding of their faith—a significant number are, anyway—and with the resources available to us today this hunger can be satisfied.

If you are a layman, you ought to insist that your church provide you with the opportunity to learn the fundamentals of the faith and that the learning process be stimulating and intellectually exciting. But make the church respect you. If the material it feeds you is prepackaged answers, then take a walk because you are getting not instruction but propaganda.

Churches have, traditionally, been reluctant to let you make up your own mind about the faith, and it will be awhile before they are willing to be completely open with their laymen. But I'm an optimist. There are signs that more and more of them are willing to inform their people instead of processing them. This is another way of saying the churches are shaking out of their sloth.

You ought to shake out of yours, too.

Chapter Thirteen

HOW TO
RATE
YOUR RELIGION

GROWING UP AS I DID in a parsonage and a churchy atmosphere, I heard plenty of conversation about various congregations of our sect, mostly about churches of which my father and his peers aspired to be pastor. These were the first-rate churches, the grade A congregations.

What was a first-rate church?

The rating had nothing whatever to do with the quality of faith exhibited by the people of the church. No one ever counted the number of bona-fide saints in the congregation when rating a church. A church was grade A if it (1) had an impressive building, (2) a membership in excess of one thousand, (3) a substantial pastoral salary, and (4) a modern, comfortable parsonage.

During my years as a pastor when I or my ministerial brethren spoke of a good church, we were employing a clerical nomenclature which meant about what my father meant by the same phrase. We had discovered that the hierarchy of our denomination assumed that a congregation which was a going concern, increasing its membership each year, paying promptly and in full the denominational assessments, keeping the church plant in good repair, and reporting healthy attendance at Sunday school and worship was a first-rate church. Statistical excellence was a reflection of the high quality of a congregation's faith. We also discovered that our MCC laymen employed the same rating system. In thirty years of pastoring MCC congregations I cannot recall any official church body, either denominational or local, attempting to assess a church's performance or a pastor's competence by any standard other than statistics.

Well, that's not quite true. Any pastor, no matter how capable, has some opposition. And when he is not vulnerable on his statistical record, the opposition will attack him on issues less amenable to statistical measurement. Yes, they say, the church is booming, but the pastor has changed the order of worship, or he doesn't preach enough about the Bible, or he discontinued the Wednesday evening prayer service. This is a kind of negative approach to the qualitative assessment of a congregation's spiritual life. But a pastor who knows how to make the mare go has nothing to fear from such attacks, whether petty and irrelevant, or whether they indicate a genuine lay concern for the congregation's quality of faith.

Is there any legitimate way to rate religion on a qualitative scale? Is it possible to say that the faith of this congregation gets an A, and that one a B, and the other one flunks?

I worried a lot about this as a pastor although to be honest I worried more about my statistical record because I knew that was the only record that counted. It is easy to be cynical about this, but we have to remember that qualitative assessment is very difficult, often arbitrary, and hard to express in the annual report. Is there healthy intellectual ferment in the congregation? Did the people end up the year with a better grasp of what their faith is all about than they had at the beginning of the year? Is the congregation learning what it means to love one another?

How can you indicate these judgments in a column of figures?

You can't.

There are, however, qualitative standards you can employ in evaluating religion. I think so, anyway. My own extensive ruminations on the subject have led me to posit three marks by which you can tell if your faith, and the faith of your congregation, is first rate. What I am setting forth as the criteria of grade A religion is a personal judgment, of course, and I am not the final arbiter of anything. But it is not an uninformed or unreflective conclusion. And, most important, I believe these criteria to be in sync with the New Testament.

1. First, does your religion major in meaning?

Now by majoring in meaning I am not referring to the catechetical approach.

Sure, you may say, we major in meaning. What do you want to know? You want to know what is man's purpose here on earth? It is "to love God and enjoy him forever." Or it is to obey God's law and win a place in paradise. Or it is to "avoid the appearance of evil."

I learned all that stuff in Sunday school, and while these reverent shibboleths sound good to the congregation when the pastor asks the questions and the children answer with the correct phrases in unison, they don't really mean anything and aren't much help in the real world.

What is the purpose of my existence? Answer the question not in grand generalities but in specifics.

How does a Christian perform as a business executive in the modern world? Don't hand me a bunch of pious simplicities such as a Christian is honest, truthful, and helpful to others. I know all that. How do I reconcile my personal integrity with the complex demands of profit, business survival, advertising, my company's ecological responsibilities, and the injustices of internecine warfare? That's what I really need to know.

What must I do to be a disciple of Christ? Don't tell me to go to church, read the Bible, and pray (which is how I recently heard a preacher define Christian discipleship to his large and flossy congregation). That's good advice, of course, but it doesn't tell me what I need to know about being a disciple in the modern world.

How does a Christian relate to the secular world? How can I determine what is God's will for my life? How should a Christian cope with his miserable marriage? What is the meaning of death? How should a Christian organize and handle the sensual life? What does it mean to be a witness for Christ? What is the relationship between my faith and my work? What does Christ mean for us today? (Bonhoeffer's question).

The Christian faith, from the beginning, has majored in meaning. It did it by clothing its meaning in grand, graphic myths. (And please, let's not quibble over the word *myth*. It isn't a dirty word. It isn't something that is untrue. A myth is a story or a legend or a poetic expression of an article of faith. Its purpose is to convey truth and meaning.) But, as any number of qualified observers have been explaining to us, the structure of Christian mythology is breaking up. The traditional Christian symbols are losing their grip on today's imagination. They no longer inform us as they once did.

We may regret that this is happening, but there is no point in denying that it is happening. It would be nice if someone would create some new clothes for Christian truth which would grab the modern imagination and convey Christian meaning as effectively as the old clothes once did. But we can't wait around for this to happen. In this interim between the passing of the old Christian myths and the arrival of new Christian myths, our job is to explain what the old ones really meant. Explaining the content of our Christian myths, something you don't have to do as long as the myths express a well-understood common belief, is how we have to go about majoring in meaning today.

For your church to major in Christian meaning requires that it be precise in its Christian language. It doesn't require that you prove the correctness of Christian affirmations because statements having to do with meaning and value are beyond proof. You can illustrate them, and you can show that they are consistent with human experience, but you can't prove them. You are, however, obligated to make it clear what you are talking about.

For example, you can't prove that we are saved by Christ. Don't waste time trying. But before I accept Christ as my savior, I want to know exactly what the New Testament means by the term *salvation*. I want to know how Christ saves me. Does salvation mean getting to heaven or escaping hell or an emotional experience or becoming a whole person or a preventive for sin or the termination of harmful personal habits, or what?

Talk to me about Jesus the Son of God, but don't tell me I have to believe it because the Angel Gabriel said it was true or that the Bible says so. Be precise. Explain to me in what sense Jesus is the Son of God, and what this means to me.

Don't assume that we are all agreed on the meaning of the word *God*. We might have been once, but no longer. Put some content into it. Give me some help on how to live out my faith in a fearfully complex society which confronts me with so many ambiguous situations. I believe that the Bible is my authority for faith and life, but lead me in understanding how it is my authority—and

124

I'm not going to let you get away with any specious and inexact answers. None of that "the Bible is God's holy word" stuff. That may be a true statement, but it is a generality. What makes it God's holy word? Who says so? How do you know? And what do you mean by God's holy word?

The whole world is in the market for meaning. And giving meaning, exploring the questions that have to do with meaning, dealing in values and priorities is Christianity's business. And that's why I make majoring in meaning my first criterion of first-rate religion.

2. Does your religion, and the religion expounded at your church, appeal to sickness or to health?

In a community where I served a number of years as pastor, there was a large, very upper-middle-class congregation whose pastor (a charming, friendly chap) enjoyed a reputation as a molder of youth. He ran his own summer youth camp, and what he did was to get these adolescents in this isolated atmosphere, subject them to a week of hell-fire preaching (bearing down especially on the horrors of sex), and turn them into hysterical repentants. I never witnessed it myself, but those who did told me the wailing was loud and the tears ran like a river.

By my lights here is a case of Christianity appealing to sickness. It is easy to exploit adolescent guilt feelings and manipulate kids, but it is a dirty trick. A normal youngster doesn't go around bewailing his sins. He probably doesn't have much real guilt to expunge anyway. You can make him sick by convincing him he's on a ski slope to hell and it's downhill all the way. You can get him to the mourner's bench and put him through the trauma of a conversion experience. The result, though, is likely to be a warped kid. Or when he gets a little maturity and is able to reflect on the experience, he'll probably be resentful for having been subjected to an embarrassing incident and acquire a distaste for all religion. I've seen it happen, over and over again.

Religion that inordinately stresses personal guilt is religion which is appealing to sickness.

Religion which promises you a spiritually elite status, with all those who are not as you are consigned to outer darkness or at least to distinct spiritual inferiority, is religion which appeals to sickness. The charismatic movement, about which I have already delivered myself, would be an example of spiritual elitism, a fact which St. Paul noted some time ago.

Religion which employs your fears to win your support is religion which appeals to sickness. You should be wary of any brand of Christianity which exploits your fears of failure, death, going to hell, communism, personal insignificance, whatever. We all have plenty of legitimate fears, and our faith should deal with them honestly—but it shouldn't exploit them.

Readily observable symptoms of sick religion are excessive narrowness, a kind of meanness of spirit (like the young preacher I mentioned earlier who spoke of the love of God with a snarl), and intellectual totalitarianism which reads out of the fellowship anyone who deviates from the spiritual party line.

There are a lot of sick people in our society. They don't need the kind of Christianity which appeals to their sickness and calls it health.

3. Is your church, your community of faith, a healing community?

The Gospels tell us to love one another, to love life, to become whole, to get well. New Testament Christianity should think of its mission as helping people to get well.

There was this church—a large, busy city church—and a young lady in the congregation discovered she had incurable cancer. Only a few people in the congregation knew about it, but the pastor and a few friends rallied to the situation. They conducted healing services with the traditional laying on of hands, but the focus of the healing ministry wasn't aimed at curing the incurable. The emphasis was on helping the woman and her husband and children and friends face the fact of her approaching death with Christian grace. This they accomplished.

I'd call that church a healing community of faith.

In your congregation or any MCC church you can think of, there are people who need all sorts of healing— cure for loneliness, frustration, despair, grief, almost any spiritual ailment you can name. Is your church like a family, closing ranks round the troubled member? Probably not. Or probably not often enough.

No church I ever served was a good example of a healing community although I made efforts, all too feeble I'm afraid, to shape them so. It takes imagination, determination, persistence to create a healing community, but mostly it takes a spirit of mutual concern. Personally, I'll overlook a church's childish theology, unaesthetic worship, and even distortions of the Bible if it is a healing community. Love one another. That's a priority.

You may want to add items to my three ways of rating a religion and rating the community of faith that religion produces. I don't claim my list is exhaustive, but I do claim it is basic. If you want a triple-A rating you have to pass this test.

Chapter Fourteen

SOME
CONSERVATIVE
CONCLUSIONS

I WAS RAISED among moderate people, trained to avoid extremes in politics, theology, and life style. My whole walk through life has been down the middle of the road, and now that I'm getting on a bit I have to watch it because I keep inching over to the right side. Bold, revolutionary thought and action are not my style. This means that my conclusions about the Middle-Class Christian and Middle-Class Christianity will be objective, at least I think they are, but they will also be influenced by my mild conservatism.

For example, I know Christians—good people, too— who hope that MC Christianity regresses to an extremely conservative, fundamentalistic stance. I don't want that. I am sufficiently acquainted with history to know that the road back is seldom the way out.

Other MCCs—also good people—would like to see MC Christianity entirely disappear. Their thesis is that it must die before the church can live again. I don't want that, either. What a waste that would be! Prodigious waste always offends those of us who were raised by the Protestant ethic.

Some Conservative Conclusions

What I want is for us to hang on to what we have, only improve it and strengthen it. That's my conservative bias.

I start with a proposition I'm pretty sure is true. It is that we MCCs are going to go right on being middle-class first and Christians second. This may be what's wrong with us. Our critics say so. But whether it's good or bad or indifferent, that's what we are going to do.

I'm not going to pull a St. Francis and found an order of indigents devoted to the care of the poor. St. Francis is one of my favorite characters in Christian history, but I'd be distressed trying to live as he lived. I'm too fond of my comfortable apartment and my color television set and my nice car and my shower and refrigerator with frozen-food section plus automatic icemaker and my king-size bed with foam-rubber mattress. If I can't reconcile my middle-classness with my Christianity, then the Christianity has to go.

You've probably never thought of it this way, have you? Not your fault. Middle-Class Christian preaching, with its Protestant ethic and all that, has obscured the idea that there could possibly be a clash between our middle-classness and our Christianity. But there could be. There is. I find the thought troubling, and you will too if you meditate on it.

The problem is that we would rather lose our chance of heaven than lose our respectability. I would. You would. The idea of my becoming some kind of religious nut trying to live his life in radical obedience to the will of God appalls me. If that's the way into the Kingdom, then there had better be a back door or I'm not going to get in, and neither are you. A harsh judgment? Maybe. But true.

We have to conclude, then, that we aren't going in for any form of faith incompatible with respectability.

The Case of a Middle-Class Christian

Let's begin there. The conclusion, however uncomfortable for us, has the merit of honesty.

From this starting point two other conclusions emerge.

1. We'd best hang on to the kind of faith and church we now have.

Such counsel will enrage those Christians who are calling for radical restructure of the church to make it conform more nearly to New Testament Christianity. I'll go along with their contention that MC Christianity doesn't resemble the religion of Jesus, or at least not very much. I doubt if Jesus would be comfortable in the average MCC worship service. I expect he would find our MCC priorities—respectability, institutional prosperity, safe and unexciting preaching, our jumble of religion and culture —all wrong. I imagine that he would lace us out, as he did the disciples, for our obtuse grasp of his gospel.

I'll even go along with the avant-garde Christians in their insistence that a radical recasting of MCC perspectives would be a good thing, that a revolutionary change in the standard-brand church is called for. But, by inspecting my own feelings, I'm aware that I am not inclined toward revolution. My middle-class nature abhors upheaval. Radical change isn't my style. You and I have too much of a spiritual investment in our MCC Christianity to chuck it out without regret. Whatever future MC Christianity has will be built on what we now have.

2. We should be more tolerant of innovation than we are.

One of my close friends is an American Baptist clergyman named Wesley Shrader. More than fifteen years ago he wrote an article for the now defunct *Life* magazine in which he called the institution of Sunday school "the most wasted hour in the week." He tells me that after all these years he still gets a lot of hostility from MC Christians because "you attacked our Sunday school."

130

Some Conservative Conclusions

As I have mentioned, the Sunday school of my boyhood was totally useless as an instrument of Christian teaching. Every church I served as pastor had a Sunday school which was, as Dr. Shrader claimed in his article, an exercise in futility. But when I tried to tamper with the Sunday school, as I always did, I banged into a rocky mountain of opposition. You would have thought that Jahweh rather than Robert Raikes had invented the Sunday school.

Here is an example, which could be multiplied, of MCC resistance to innovation. It is an example of misguided conservatism.

If we are going to be conservatives, and we are, then we ought to be sound, sensible conservatives. And sensible conservatives are tolerant of innovation, even of innovations which do not appeal to them personally.

However, I have a considerable confidence in the flexibility of the MCC nature. Middle-class America believes in progress. It is more reluctant to accept innovation in religion than in its economics, politics, and education, but it will accept innovation in religion when it is convinced that an innovation is progress.

Some of the innovations which are already on the scene you might as well get used to because I'm pretty sure they are going to be around for awhile.

For example, there is a deemphasis of what has been called "placed Christianity."

That is, there is and there will be less interest in fabulous buildings, showy institutions, socially prestigious congregations, vast parochial school systems, and so on. This kind of Christianity is expensive to maintain, requires most of a congregation's energy for housekeeping (raising the budget, looking after the plant, recruiting enough members to prevent institutional decline), and appears to have limited attraction for the young.

The Case of a Middle-Class Christian

A concomitant of the decline of placed Christianity seems to be a marked increase in small, informal Christian fellowships.

Some of these "house churches" will be held together by a leading personality, some by emphasizing a particular theological perspective, some by a commitment to a special mission. My own feeling is that where large congregations with big church plants survive they will include a variety of these small fellowships within their memberships, churches within the church. There is nothing very new about this, of course. What is new is the burgeoning popularity of the small Christian fellowship. I think this is a healthy trend, and were I pastor of a large congregation today, I would do everything I could do to encourage it.

Another innovation is the increase in "tentmaker clergy."

By this I mean that there are, and there will be, more and more ministers who earn their living at a secular profession. One of the nation's largest standard-brand seminaries, I am told, is now encouraging its students to fit themselves for a secular profession. My own denomination (United Methodist), which has traditionally been chary of the idea that an ordained clergyman could exercise a legitimate ministry outside the parish or hierarchy, has recently made provisions for the tentmaker ministry. The idea of the tentmaker ministry is as old as St. Paul, and I see much promise in its resuscitation. For one thing, it is easier to be a prophetic voice when your bread and butter are not dependent on pleasing a congregation. Also, when a minister works in the secular world, he helps erase the image of the clergyman as a "kept man." And a tentmaker clergyman has much freedom to decide where and in what manner he will exercise his ministry.

It looks, too, as if we are going to see more and more interdenominational cooperation and less and less preoccupation with denominational merger.

Here is an example of MCC conservatism blending with innovation. Denominational mergers are cumbersome procedures and seldom live up to their advance notices. Sectarian rivalry was—and still is to some extent—a Christian scandal. Sectarian cooperation should be sped along with every assist we can give it. Denominational labels are not the barriers to unity they once were, though, and the evolutionary process of learning to work together without abandoning the labels is more compatible with the MCC character than fusing ourselves into a few supersects or even one huge ecclesiastical organization.

Many of us will feel threatened by these and other changes in the familiar patterns of our MC Christianity. We are likely to be troubled by the continuing shrinkage in church membership, attendance at Sunday school and worship, and decline in contributions. It is easy to be nervous these days about the future of Middle-Class Christianity.

It's going to be different, that's for sure. When someone asks me if I have confidence in the future of the church, I have to answer, "If you mean do I have confidence that the church in its present forms and configurations will persist, no, I don't. Christians have expressed their faith in all sorts of styles, forms, and organizational structures throughout the history of the church. Our American denominational Middle-Class Christian parish is a relatively modern example of organizing the community of faith. We should not regard it as normative, permanent, or sacred. We have every reason, though, to be optimistic about the persistence of the Christian community. So long as there are people who see in Jesus Christ the clue to the meaning of human existence, they will get together and create a community of faith. That's all we need to know to retain our confidence in the future of the church."

Chapter Fifteen

WAS
JESUS
AN
EXISTENTIALIST?

I GREW UP A PLATONIST. I believed that essence precedes existence. I did not know I was a Platonist—indeed, I scarcely heard the name *Plato* before I went to college, let alone knew what he taught. And if you had asked me what "essence precedes existence" meant, I would have favored you with a blank stare.

But I was a Platonist nonetheless because Middle-Class Christians then were mostly Platonists—and they still are. Plato taught that only ideas are real and permanent, that what we think of as real—a chair, a pet dog—are imperfect representations of the idea of a chair or a pet dog. Christians early found Plato's philosophy congenial, and adapted it to Christian thought. The real and the permanent exists in the mind of God, they said.

So, nearly two thousand years later in a little Indiana town, I was taught that God has in mind that I should behave in certain specific ways. Since God doesn't change his mind, these laws of behavior never vary, are the same for everyone, and are unalterable by situations and circumstances. Essence (the ideas which determine what my values should be and what kind of character I should

134

have) precedes my existence (those ideas have been there
all the time since before the foundations of the earth
were laid). We didn't talk about essence and existence at
the Methodist church in Windfall, Indiana, of course. We
talked about the Ten Commandments and the Sermon on
the Mount as God's law. We learned that it was our duty
to mold our character by strict conformity to these moral
and behavioral patterns which were eternal in the heavens.
If we deviated, there was forgiving grace, of course. But
deviation was sin, always sin. And that's how I became
a Platonist, though unaware that that was the name for
what I was.

Most Middle-Class Christians still carry this concept of
reality around in their heads. It goes something like this:

The universe first existed in the mind of God. The universe, with all the laws that govern its existence and operation, is a replica of God's thoughts. In addition to the
physical universe there is what we might call the moral
universe, the universe of moral and ethical values. This
universe, though not so easily perceived and observed as
the physical universe, is nonetheless just as real as the
physical universe. Since you can't see it as you can see a
star through a telescope or measure it as you can measure
bacteria under a microscope, God has revealed it to us
through Scripture and Jesus Christ. The laws of the moral
universe are just as precise, just as binding on us as the
laws of the physical universe. We do not invent moral
and ethical laws any more than we invented the law of
gravity. They are there to be discovered and obeyed. Like
the physical universe, the moral universe is a replica of
God's thoughts. Man's obligation is to obey those laws,
just as he'd better observe the law of gravity or else.

Conceiving the world of morals and values as analogous
to the physical world has immense appeal to us. We like
precision, and we like certainty. By applying the laws of

the physical universe to the problems of daily living we have fashioned a phenomenally successful technology. Does it not stand to reason, then, that the correct employment of the laws governing morals and values will issue in a correspondingly successful ethical technology?

If you will reflect on it, you will see that not only have I described what you as a Middle-Class Christian in all probability believe, but that this vision of the moral universe is the regnant ethical vision in the Christian world today. The Roman Catholic church maintains a vast system of ecclesiastical courts whose function is to apply the moral law in specific situations. This vision is the stated or unstated assumption underlying most Protestant sermons.

But it has been challenged. A school of thought, a secular philosophy which has come to be called existentialism, has challenged the vision. Existentialism turns Plato around. "Existence precedes essence," it says.

Practically, this means that you do not discover moral and ethical laws inherent in the universe because there are none to discover. Whereas the Christian (Platonic) view holds that your freedom is limited to accepting or rejecting the life values which exist in the mind of God, the existentialist claims that you, and you alone, choose what shall be the values which shape your life. The idea of a universally binding moral law is absurd. Your essence (your character, what you believe to be meaningful for you, your personal values) is wrought out on the anvil of your experience, your unique existence. Traditional Christianity says to you, "Conform." Existentialism says to you, "Choose for yourself."

My inclination, when I first heard of the existentialist challenge to my Christian vision of a fixed and precise moral universe, was to dismiss it as nonsense. I feel certain that this is the inclination of most Middle-Class Christians. What kind of a topsy-turvy moral world would I be living in without a clear and detailed set of values by which to check my performance? How could anyone know he was good unless he had the rules of goodness to guide him?

But these, I came to see, were the wrong questions. If I am going to be a Christian, the only relevant question for me is, Was Jesus a Platonist or an existentialist?

The answer is, I think, that Jesus was both a Platonist and an existentialist, but that the way in which Jesus lived more nearly resembled the style of the existentialist than the style of the Platonist.

Consider, for example, how Jesus rejected the orthodox Judaism of his day, which was a highly developed moral technology.

Middle-Class Christians usually cheer this rejection. Pharisee is a bad word in our lexicon. But what we think Jesus did was to abolish an old, bad moral technology and substitute a new, good moral technology. He wiped out one book of rules, we think, and replaced it with another. And that is why so many of us Middle-Class Christians bear a startling resemblance in spirit and outlook to the Pharisees Jesus rejected.

Apparently Jesus rejected Pharisaic legalistic morality because he thought it produced the wrong kind of people.

There is no question that a thoroughgoing moral technocrat will think in terms of moral minimums (how much do I have to do to qualify as good?). He will be hard put to avoid pride (I measure up to God's law, but you don't). And he can hardly avoid narrowness of spirit because enlarging his moral horizons threatens his already achieved moral acceptability.

Sound like anybody you know?

But if Jesus believed that a highly developed moral technology like Pharisaic Judaism (and by implication any Christian version of Pharisaism) was bad for people, then what is good for people? Was he, after all, an existentialist?

Jesus couldn't have been an existentialist. A true existentialist says, "There are no clues to what is good. There are no values except as you see them as values. There is no guide to character and behavior outside yourself."

Jesus didn't talk like this at all. He said there is a clue to the values with which you should structure your life. It is the character of God. God is loving (a nonsentimental concern for every person), compassionate, and merciful. If God is like this, then you should be too. After that, you are on your own. You can't develop this perspective into a moral technology because you could lay out ten million rules for it, but tomorrow morning a situation will arise which isn't covered by the rules. Besides, keeping rules isn't a very good motive for being good. When Jesus told the Parable of the Good Samaritan he was establishing a model for Christian values in action. You start with the values of love and compassion and mercy, and do what you have to do.

So maybe we should say that Jesus was a semiexistentialist. He did believe in a fixed and eternal moral guide or obligation (I hesitate to call it a moral law because that has a forbidding tone quite at odds with the nature of love and compassion and mercy). But, like the existentialist, he seemed to believe that you achieve essence, you form your character, and you choose your particular values in the context of your own, your unique existence.

This picture of Christian values and Christian behavior is growing in popularity. A few years ago it got quite a bit of publicity through the secular press under the name of *situation ethics*. There are varieties of situation ethics, of course. In general, however, situation ethics holds that in any given situation "the most good" and "the least evil" are synonymous. It values Christian laws and rules as good for instructional purposes and to be observed in circumstances where their observation fulfills love and mercy. They are to be overridden, however, when they frustrate or do not fulfill them, as is frequently the case.

Situation ethics generates antagonistic reactions in Middle-Class Christians, at least at first. It did in me. It isn't neat. It takes too much responsibility off of God and puts too much on me. I can never have that comforting certainty that I am absolutely right, that I have strained hard and fulfilled the law. It makes me think hard all the time about my value judgments, my personal behavior, instead of just checking with the rule book before I act. Situation ethics simply isn't as convenient as my old Platonic view.

Nonetheless, I have come to believe that this sort of Christian semiexistentialism is on the right track. I believe it for two reasons:

1. This Christian semiexistentialism seems to me more congruent with reality, less artificial, than a highly spelled-out Christian moral technology.

It is our nature, of course, to want to cover all ethical bases. Our position is more defensible (and personally more comforting) if we can confidently cite the law or rule which specifies what our behavior should be in any situation.

Actually, this can't be done. Life isn't like that. It is always out ahead of us. It is always eliciting from us the amazed exclamation, "I never thought of that!" So why pretend we have covered all bases? Why not admit that we haven't, we can't, life won't let us, and rely on an approach to values and Christian behavior which will guide us in all situations?

2. This Christian semiexistentialism seems likely to me to produce a better kind of person than a developed Christian legalism will produce.

The Case of a Middle-Class Christian

This, of course, is a value judgment on my part. There is no way to prove that the Pharisaic personality is worse than a more open, tolerant, less narrow, and less prideful personality. It's just that I like the more open person better than I do the Pharisee. Evidently Jesus did too.

One thing is certain—we are all existentialists in that we choose our values. Your values may be all fixed eternally in the heavens, but you chose them. You could have chosen others. I have come to believe, quite contrary to what I began believing, that when it comes to personal values, moral values, ethical values, it is entirely a matter of choice. There just isn't any way to prove that my values are better than the next guy's values. I inherited my Middle-Class Christian values, to be sure. But my present Christian perspective is my choice. Oh, to be sure, I am influenced by my upbringing, traditions, mind set. But I am very conscious of my freedom to choose or reject my values.

But I can't prove that my values are the only values or even the best values. I choose to be a Christian. Jesus Christ teaches me that the clue to value and the guide for my behavior is the character of God. But I accept this as a revelation, not as a proof. Remember, you have to call things by their right names.

Still, we Christians find it hard to refrain from developing ethical systems from the teachings of Jesus. Jesus' ethical teachings are fragmentary, and usually uttered in the context of some life situation with which he was confronted (the existential style), and do not lend themselves to development as a moral technology.

But we keep trying to do it. Middle-Class Christians are wont to look on the Beatitudes as a guidebook for Christians, a list of distinctively Christian laws for personal behavior, Jesus' ethical system. But they aren't any of these things.

Was Jesus an Existentialist?

When you choose to be a Christian, you choose to live in a value atmosphere which isn't at all like a legal system. Joachim Jeremias, a distinguished New Testament scholar, tells us the difference in this passage from his commentary on the Sermon on the Mount:

The Sermon on the Mount is not law, but gospel . . . this is the difference between law and gospel: the law leaves man to rely on his own strength and challenges him to do his utmost. The gospel, on the other hand, brings man before the gift of God and challenges him really to make the inexpressible gift of God the basis for his life. Those are two different worlds. In order to make the difference clear one should avoid the terms "Christian ethic," "Christian morality," "Christian morals," because these secular expressions are inadequate and liable to misunderstanding. Instead of these one should speak of a "lived faith." Then it is clearly stated that the gift of God precedes His demands.

The sayings of Jesus which have been collected in the Sermon on the Mount are not intended to lay a legal yoke upon Jesus' disciples. . . . Rather, these sayings of Jesus delineate the lived faith. They say: you are forgiven; you are a child of God; you belong to His Kingdom. The sun of righteousness has risen over your life . . . you belong to the city of God, the light of which shines in the darkness.

Chapter Sixteen

THE CASE
IS
STILL OPEN

I RECALL THAT AS A CHILD I attended, or, more accurately, was taken to, the regular midweek prayer service of the churches my father pastored. I suppose that my mother, expected as the pastor's wife to be there, took my brother and me because there wasn't anything else to do with us.

Now an old-fashioned prayer and testimony service is not designed for children, and I know that I was unutterably bored. But one impression, absorbed through my pores perhaps, remains with me to this day. The faithful, in prayer and especially in testimony, reiterated one theme. They had seen the light at some date now long past (only middle-aged and elderly people attended these devotionals). The truth had been vouchsafed them and, praise God, they hadn't had a doubt since or changed their minds one iota in all the intervening years. This undeviating intellectual loyalty to every crossed *t* and dotted *i* in the content of their faith, they confidently asserted, was the Christian's sword and buckler in the daily battle with the world, the flesh, and the devil, and also sweet incense in the nostrils of Jehovah.

There are, no doubt, many Christians who still think

142

this way. Well, if they are right, then I am wrong, and all these questionings, all these rethinkings, signify nothing but my personal shortage of godly credulity—for which, presumably, I will be docked by the recording angel. I, of course, think I'm right. Or at least, I plead that I could not help the nagging questions or avoid all that pondering over my inherited Middle-Class Christianity.

But what good did it do me? Is the place where I am now better than the place where I was when I started? Any honest assessment requires, at a minimum, a brief comparison of my two states of faith.

If you were to observe me in church some Sunday, you would put me down for a typical Middle-Class Christian. I'm about the same, on the outside, as I have always been. I might wear a sports jacket to church these days, unthinkable a few years ago. But it is the times, not I, who have changed.

I would say the creeds along with you, and I wouldn't have my mental fingers crossed. I would, however, mean some parts to be taken by the Almighty as a symbol of what I believed rather than a literal recital of my faith.

I would sing the hymns enthusiastically although I might wince at some of the words here and there.

I would appreciate the sermon if it was well done although I likely would criticize it for errors and other deficiencies afterward. But then, I've always done that.

As I say, from the outside I don't look any different from what I have always been—a Middle-Class Christian who finds his community of faith in a standard-brand American denomination.

Inside, though, I'm a lot different.

Look at all the luggage of inherited faith I have abandoned.

I have rejected the notion of a three-story universe,

with heaven up there and hell down there, with the purpose of my existence to escape one and get to the other.

I have rejected much that I was taught about God, especially God as fundamentally a stern righteous judge.

I have abandoned my early confidence that my faith furnished me with precise rules for any and all of life's situations and that the Christian life consists in rigid and literal application of these rules.

I no longer believe that God requires or especially wants me to be faithful to some respectable middle-class organized church. That I go to a respectable middle-class organized church is because of my tastes and habits rather than a divine mandate.

Years ago I jettisoned the business of identifying middle-class American cultural values and the national aspirations and endeavors of the United States with the will of God. I am aware that this kind of Christianity is what sociologists call civil religion and that some of these sociologists say we need a civil religion if we are to have a healthy nation. But I'm not buying it. Once I did, but not any more.

My early Christian education taught me that Christian moral and ethical precepts, Christian rules for living as spelled out in the Decalogue and the Beatitudes, can be proved to be superior to any other ethical perspective. I do not think this is so. The rightness or wrongness of moral and ethical values is not amenable to proof. You choose the values you choose because of reasons which seem persuasive to you.

For a long time I believed that God wants us to depend on his aid to get us safely through life and that he'll see us safely through if we please him. Now I believe he expects us to take our chances and depend on ourselves.

I was brought up to believe that salvation is God's method for getting me into heaven. Now I believe it means God's wish that I become a whole person.

The above is only a partial list.

What has happened to me as I have given up many items of the faith I inherited is not so much a profound change but a shift in emphasis. I have moved away from a strict, closed, supernatural revelationism (if there is such a word) and have moved toward what I will call a kind of worldly Christian humanism.

Where once I saw man and man's concerns divided into the material and the spiritual, I now see that this is a phony separation, certainly not biblical, assuredly unsanctioned by Jesus. The flesh and the spirit are all of a part. This means that pious exercises are in no way superior to the thankful enjoyment of a good meal.

The world, then, is not an enemy of the spiritual life as I had been taught that it was. The world is a gift. It is the environment in which God has chosen to set us. We achieve what we achieve in it, not somewhere else. The Kingdom is here now, in part anyway. I find the clues for living my life in the world, for finding my way into the Kingdom, in Jesus Christ. That's why he came. That's how he saves me.

I know that the words *worldly* and *humanism* offend many good Christians. They think of them as bad words. I think of them as good words. *Worldly* simply means focusing our interests on our life in the world and how best to live it. *Humanism* is shorthand for saying that human values are preeminent values. Where's the conflict here with the Bible? What's to argue about?

If *conservative* and *liberal* are the only adjectives denoting shades of a Christian's orientation, then I have moved away from the conservative and toward the liberal interpretation of the faith. However, these adjectives are apt to be confusing in these days of religious turbulence. They once meant something specific, perhaps, but now they have become stereotypes, and stereotypes contribute little in our understanding of one another.

The Case of a Middle-Class Christian

I certainly do not boast that I am a liberal Christian. However, if liberal means that I take seriously the information I get from science, philosophy, biblical scholarship, theology, sociology, and so on, then I am one. If it means that human values take precedence over creeds, ideologies, and schematic salvation formulas, then call me a liberal. If a liberal Christian is one who chooses to depend on reason as well as revelation for faith information, then I choose to be a liberal Christian. I expect, even though you may think of yourself as a conservative Christian, you pretty much agree with me. I know this because I know from experience that Middle-Class Christians tend, on the whole, to be reasonable and compassionate people.

I recall an instance involving a leading layman in a church I once served as pastor. This fellow boasted about his conservatism—in politics, economics, and religion he was, by his own frequent admission, a thrice-dipped, fully certified fundamentalist. Once, though, he talked to me about a minister-friend of his who had been treated rather roughly by the hierarchy of the church. The church was, by its laws, correct in what it had done. Its treatment of the minister had been for what it deemed the best interests of the institution. Any true conservative would have agreed that the church had done the right thing. But this conservative layman said to me, "What they did to my friend was an affront to human dignity, and to affront human dignity is simply unchristian." In the crunch, what he really believed vanquished his professed ideology. Conservative Christians and liberal Christians are more alike than they think they are.

But, that aside, am I any better off for all the questioning of my inherited faith?

I think I am.

Admittedly, my present position is not something new

or startling. A goodly number of Christians arrived at this approximate position long before I was on the scene, and millions share it. I could have read about it in a book and saved myself the trouble of the questing.

The important thing for me, though, is that I arrived where I arrived by my own journey, not someone else's. I wrestled with these faith questions myself. What I believe now is not what someone else told me I ought to believe. It is what I can believe on my own as a result of having thought it out myself. And what you believe as a result of having done your own homework is stronger than what you believe from cribbing someone else's homework.

Also, I think I'm better off for having taken the trip because it was a liberating experience.

The Christianity I inherited, meritorious on some scores as it may have been, was spiritually constricting. It had all the answers. It was a closed system. It saw no moral or spiritual ambiguities which would not yield to the application of simple copybook prescriptions. It was—or pretended to be—a closed-end faith, complete and adequate as it stood. This kind of religion, productive of certainty and a sense of spiritual security to be sure, also narrows the spirit and stultifies the soul.

Jesus talked a lot about liberation—freeing the prisoners, disentangling the soul from the religious red tape of Pharisaic Judaism, eliminating the hindering loyalties to empty tradition which were responsible for so much of the spiritual grubbiness he saw all about him. Any movement of the spirit away from narrowness and mean boundaries toward openness and abundance seems to me consonant with the teachings of Jesus. So I count my experience of liberation a Christian dividend.

Most important, I suppose, I couldn't live with the faith I inherited, and I can with the faith I have now. What I inherited didn't provide me with a structure of belief, a

147

faith stance with which to live in the modern world. What I have now does.

Some people will say, no doubt, "Well, your religion is too rational, too cool. Religion is more than reason. It has to do with inspiration, and ecstasy, and soarings of the spirit."

I didn't say it didn't.

All I'm saying is that you'd best begin with facts, evidence, data. Get a firm grasp on the known before sailing off into the unknown. Religious faith is finally a venture, but it need not initially be a venture. Like Nero Wolfe said, your surmises should stand on the legs of fact.

We are all different, a statement that ranks low in originality but is often forgotten by good Christian people promulgating the faith. They often act as if we must all respond to the evangelical plea in only one way.

But some people are credulous by nature and find it easy to believe. Others have to look over any proposition, no matter how holy, look over it with care before they accept it. Most of us, I'm afraid—credulous or inquisitive— are predisposed to believe what we want to believe, and we should keep this disconcerting fact about ourselves in mind whenever we are striking faith stances.

One thing we should all realize is that the Christian faith is open-ended. New light will be coming in. More news about the nature of the universe, which is news about the nature of God, arrives daily. Our knowledge about ourselves, the kind of creatures we are, is expanding, which means that our knowledge of God is expanding. Newly discovered manuscripts, better translations of the Bible, better methods of critical study furnish us fresh information about Jesus and the origin of our faith.

So, if this book has any evangelical purpose, it is not to persuade you to believe as I believe, but to urge you to be an open-ended Christian. I urge you because I am

148

convinced that faith has to be consistent with our knowledge of the world and our experience in it. If religious faith doesn't have to square with knowledge and be consistent with experience, then it is a purely private devotionalism, a thing apart from real life and not to be taken seriously by anyone but the holder.

Jesus expected his religion to be taken seriously. He said he had new light to bring. He insisted that much of what passed for religion in his time didn't make any sense, but the new light he brought did make sense. He said that those who were open to this new light would find liberation and fulfillment.

I believe this.